HIS VOICE
in My Heart

Lori J. O'Neil

Lori O'Neil

2020

Nation of Women
PUBLISHING

"His Voice in My Heart"
ISBN # 978-1-7341545-7-3

Published by Nation of Women Publishing, Fort Worth, Texas 76114

Printed in United States of America. All rights reserved under International Copyright Law.

Cover Design: Rachel Mayer

Section Listing

Dedication

Written in dedication to Paula Hemgesberg.

She walked me through the hard stuff when I needed someone to understand, but she didn't just sympathize. Paula gave comfort but seemed to know when I needed the tough love of reality—the wakeup call. Those times, though few, were sometimes hard to take, but I knew that she loved me and I trusted her. I knew that if she needed to dish out tough love, I had better look deeper within to figure out why.

Paula has the wisdom of God to unravel confusion and reknit it into a beautiful picture of understanding.

Thank you, Paula, for sticking by me when it felt like my world had walked away. I am forever thankful for your mentoring and friendship. You demonstrate His Love with incredible patience and I praise God for you!

May all be BLESSED to know the Mercy and Grace of Jesus, the Compassionate Love of the Father, the Gentle Comfort of the Holy Spirit, and a wonderful friend like Paula.

Introduction

As I began to sort messages for my first book, 'Comfort in the Challenge,' one word, as a voice, arose big in my heart, *prisoners*. I sensed this additional assignment was to be a special book and paid close attention to set aside messages for it.

You may not know a prisoner and yet you may be one. You see a prisoner isn't always behind bars. Many are imprisoned in their own heart. You may be functioning on the outside, but inside are imprisoned by thoughts, fear, heartache, and loss. Feelings begin to take control and that list grows, as does the pain of one abused, neglected, and broken of heart.

He came to set the captives free!

I listened as His Voice in my heart guided me in the order of placement for each message. Over a span of many years, the Lord has spoken to me on many subjects, but now it is clear that He has been speaking a journey. From the very first message, you find that He created you special and none other like YOU. He has a purpose for you, that only you can fill. He never lost sight of you, but the pressures of life, wounds and the like, have blocked you from seeing Him; blocked you from knowing and fulfilling your purpose.

Take the journey.

I have known these messages, but as I read them through, His Compassion for you in my heart became so great that I was overcome with tears—He loves you so much!

'His Voice in My Heart' is a journey that speaks the Heart of God, His Love, and His purpose for you. In it you will find messages to heal, confirm and deepen your relationship IN HIM. They are not meant to replace the Word, but serve to amplify it, as fresh bread.

You may not struggle in life, but know of one who does. 'His Voice in My Heart' will give insight into the journey of another; deepening your understanding of what they face; allowing His compassion to fill your heart.

Scriptures are added to verify the messages, for He will not veer from His Word. Those referenced without parenthesis are a direct quote; while those in parenthesis are added to amplify and clarify a sentence or paragraph nearby. Scriptures are given at the bottom of the page as well, for those who wish further study of the Word.

Listen, as He speaks to you *personally*. A journey begins, but it's only the beginning of a *lifetime* of *freedom* that He has for you, as you study His Word and listen to *hear*, 'His Voice in My Heart.'

Show Your ID

It is amazing that, even though I created man to be unique and individual, so many are desperately trying to be like someone else. I created you special, and put My stamp of approval on you—your fingerprint. No two are alike; every day more are created, yet none duplicated.

Why?

Because I wanted you and no other like you. I purposed you and none other for your purpose. Through the ages, many are called, but no one has the exact same call—no duplicates means no mistakes.

Twins look the same to the world if they are identical. You may fool the world, as they say, but I AM not of this world and I AM not a fool. Man looks on the outward appearance—

I look on the heart!

I see who you are, not what you look like. I AM the author and finisher of your faith and the lover of your soul. I reject no one, for you are irreplaceable—uniquely you! Therefore, My question to you is . . .

Why?

Why, in a world teeming with people, do you feel insignificant when I know right where you are at all times? I never stop thinking about you. My eye is ever upon you. You will never have another fingerprint and no one will ever have yours.

Why then would you not want to leave a footprint that is just as unique?

Be you.

If you want to imitate someone, imitate Me. For I AM never the same to two individuals—I AM unique to you, and My footprint I gladly give to you, as I gave you My Life.

Be uniquely you and come, follow Me.

Bring along your fingerprint—you'll need some ID.

Follow Me.

"—for the Lord sees not as man sees; man looks on the outward appearance, but the Lord looks on the heart." I Samuel 16:7b

"For we are his workmanship, created in Christ Jesus for good works, which God prepared beforehand, that we should walk in them." Ephesians 2:10

"Therefore be imitators of God, as beloved children. And walk in love, as Christ loved us and gave himself up for us, a fragrant offering and sacrifice to God." Ephesians 5:1-2

~ Psalms 139:1-18 ~ Jeremiah 1:5a ~ Ephesians 1:3-6 ~

Abide and Conquer

Loneliness seems to plague man, in a world that becomes ever more secluded; in contrast to My plan for family and community.

I created man to love—an expression of Myself—to give love and receive love; and yet so many seek or fall into isolation, declining for lack of love. Why?

Why, in a world so teeming with life, would you avoid life?

Why, in your hunger for love, would you reject love?

You have armored yourself against love for fear of rejection, fear of hurt, and the unknown. But what you haven't known is Me, for perfect love casts out fear. (I John 4:18)

I AM perfect Love.

If in Me you abide, you are never alone. Though man may reject, I will never neglect the one who seeks to know Me. (Jeremiah 29:11-13)

Know Me on the inside—not from afar.

From afar I AM only Deity, one you don't understand. Invite Me inside and we will abide, and you may call Me friend. (Psalms 25:14) (John 14:23)

Never alone.

Then you will understand that it is the work of the enemy to divide and conquer. But you can *abide* and *conquer* him—conquer fear with love, for perfect love casts out fear.

Have no fear—Perfect Love is here—

I AM Perfect Love.

"I will not leave you desolate; I will come to you. Yet a little while, and the world will see me no more, but you will see me; because I live, you will live also. In that day you will know that I am in my Father, and you in me, and I in you. He who has my commandments and keeps them, he it is who loves me; and he who loves me will be loved by my Father, and I will love him and manifest myself to him." John 14:18-21

~ John 15:10-17 ~ I John 4:7-8 ~

No Shame

Tender is My heart toward those who have been shamed—My child, it should not be so. You are a pearl of great price, the reason I gave My life; no greater gift could I offer you.

I take your pain.

I've lived your shame.

Please let Me heal your heart and give you a fresh new start.

I cannot undo what has been done, but I can heal the wounds and give you new life for the old. I can remove bitterness and, in exchange, bring forgiveness.

Trust Me.

Pour out your heart before Me, and then listen while I speak words of tenderness—words of love to heal. If you will cease to blame, I will take the shame. As you learn to forgive, I will give you favor and honor and fill you with gladness. (Matthew 6:14-15) (Psalms 84:11-12)

But first, My love, we must remove you from the madness . . .

Come away from it and embrace new life; receive My love and put an end to strife! Shame no longer has power over you—

When you know who you are,

and

Him who loves you!

I AM HE

"The Spirit of the Lord God is upon me, because the Lord has anointed me to bring good tidings to the afflicted; he has sent me to bind up the brokenhearted, to proclaim liberty to the captives, and the opening of the prison to those who are bound; to proclaim the year of the Lord's favor, and the day of vengeance of our God; to comfort all who mourn; to grant to those who mourn in Zion—to give them a garland instead of ashes, the oil of gladness instead of mourning, the mantle of praise instead of a faint spirit; that they may be called oaks of righteousness, the planting of the Lord, that he may be glorified." Isaiah 61:1-3

"There is therefore now no condemnation for those who are in Christ Jesus." Romans 8:1

"But thou, O Lord, art a shield about me, my glory, and the lifter of my head." Psalms 3:3

"O Lord, thou wilt hear the desire of the meek; thou wilt strengthen their heart, thou wilt incline thy ear to do justice to the fatherless and the oppressed, so that man who is of the earth may strike terror no more." Psalms 10:17-18

~ Psalms 9:9-10 ~ Isaiah 61:7 ~ Psalms 5:11-12 ~

The Royal Visit
A True Testimony

In a gathering of believers one night, as I worshipped with eyes closed, I saw Jesus walk in. I did not see Him with my physical eyes, but in the spirit. I could see Him as clearly as if my eyes were open, if not clearer.

As we worshipped in a large open circle, He entered in. Jesus was dressed in a beautiful, royal robe that was purple and trimmed in white fur all around. Standing in front of each worshipper, He cupped the sides of their face gently with His hands; taking time to study each face as He slowly made His way around the room.

When finished, Jesus strode purposely to the center of His circle of honor and threw His arms and fisted hands up in a stance of power and triumphant victory! I can still see it to this day— forever recorded on my heart.

At the end of worship, everyone sat down for a time of sharing and reflection. Anyone that cared to share, came forth with their experience of the worship. As I sat there listening to each one, a woman excitedly reported that she had seen Jesus walk in. This caught my attention, so I leaned forward, listening carefully to every word. When she had finished, I casually asked her what He was wearing. I about fell of my chair as she animatedly replied, emphasizing her words with her hands, "Oh, He was all decked out in a purple robe that was trimmed with white fur all around." She had witnessed what I had seen, exactly!

I leaped off my chair, too excited to hold still, and exclaimed— "I saw Him too!" There were a few that seemed upset that they had not witnessed His visit as well. He certainly does not play favorites. I don't know the reason that they had not, but maybe they were not prepared to receive that night. I do know this—a worship meeting is not the time to *begin* to prepare. Each should come *ready*, built up in the spirit and having cast all cares aside—*ready*—to honor Jesus!

A House of Glass

The structure would not be the same for a building of steel, as that of a building of glass; one would seem stronger, and yet it takes greater strength to be transparent.

It is easy to hide behind a façade—as steel, to harden thy face without the slightest trace of emotion or love. But that is a lonely place to be, always hiding—even from Me.

Oh, can't you see?

That it is love that draws others near—Love that stops the fear in a heart that feels split apart. The cries of a hurting soul reach My ears...

"The eyes of the Lord are toward the righteous, and his ears toward their cry." Psalms 34:15

I'm right here.

I wait for you to see clear, and step out from the house you hold dear; that shell, the lie that holds you there.

Your heart stands still.

Until

Allow Me to be revealed in thee.

Allow Me to transform the condition of your heart—to give you a brand-new start, and a house that is strong; not made from steel, but what you can feel—

Love.

A love that changes that house of steel to glass—relationship at last!

Love

It's how I see you.

"But God, who is rich in mercy, because of His great love with which He loved us, even when we were dead in trespasses, made us alive together with Christ (by grace you have been saved), and raised us up together, and made us sit together in the heavenly places in Christ Jesus, that in the ages to come He might show the exceeding riches of His grace in His kindness toward us in Christ Jesus." Eph 2:4-7 NKJV

"O righteous Father, the world has not known you, but I have known thee; and these know that thou hast sent me. I made it known to them thy name, and I will make it known, that the love with which thou hast loved me may be in them, and I in them." John 17:25-26

"If you keep my commandments, you will abide in my love, just as I have kept my Father's commandments and abide in his love. These things I have spoken to you, that my joy may be in you, and that your joy may be full." John 15:10-11

"A new heart I will give you, and a new spirit I will put within you; and I will take out of your flesh the heart of stone and give you a heart of flesh." Ezekiel 36:26

~ John 14:27 ~ Jeremiah 31:3 ~

I Approve

Many spend their entire lives seeking approval from a parent or other family member. They toil and strive only to *survive* their life, but never to *thrive*.

Stop right where you are. I want you to know—

- ❖ For Now
- ❖ For Always
- ❖ I APPROVE

You have never had to 'measure up' to My love. My love is *always* there for you. You don't have to 'say' the right thing, nor 'do' the right thing. There is nothing that you do to *earn* Me but—

- ❖ Receive My Love.
- ❖ Receive My Blood, shed for you.
- ❖ Wear My Crown.

My Blood clothes you in righteousness—right-standing with the Father. It just doesn't get any better than that!

"There is therefore now no condemnation for those who are in Christ Jesus." Romans 8:1

"Therefore, if anyone is in Christ, he is a new creation; the old has passed away, behold, the new has come." II Corinthians 5:17

"Fear not, little flock, for it is your Father's good pleasure to give you the kingdom." Luke 12:32

"For the kingdom of God is not food and drink but righteousness and peace and joy in the Holy Spirit; he who thus serves Christ is acceptable to God and approved by men. Let us then pursue what makes for peace and for mutual upbuilding." Romans 14:17-19

The Color of Love
A True Testimony

One evening, during worship with a group of believers, I was caught away in the spirit. Like Paul, "Whether in the body or out of the body, I do not know." (II Corinthians 12:2) What I do know is that this vision was one in which I participated, in living color, and I felt the warmth of the sun on my face.

I was taken to a place that appeared to be Africa. The sun was very hot, a cloudless day. I watched as a man, the color of blackest ebony, squatted down next to a lake. Cupping water in his hands, he poured it over his head and onto his strong, muscular back. The sun shimmered glistening hot, as I watched the small amount of water trickle down, finding its path.

Abruptly, I found myself in an Indian village. There a young Indian girl was being readied for what looked to be a coming-of-age ceremony. She wore a beautifully beaded, light-doeskin dress, and was being fitted with an elaborate headdress. Amongst much excited activity, I noticed an old, old, Indian Chief, sitting cross-legged on the ground, next to the opening of his teepee. His face was papery brown and so wrinkled it looked as if another could not find its place on his face. He was solemn as he sat there motionless, silently observing the progress of the women.

Then, just as suddenly, I appeared to be in India, and there witnessed an Indian man dressed entirely in white; a cloth turban wrapped his head. He sat at the edge of a cement-encased pool, his pantlegs pulled up, baring lower legs and feet as he dangled them in the water.

It seemed as if only moments spent at each place, just enough to observe what was happening. Lastly, I found myself standing before a giant wooden cross. Majestically, it stood against a clear blue sky and bright sunshine. Next to me, Jesus, stood with a small newborn baby in His hands. He held the baby face-up across His open palms held tightly together. The baby's little legs and arms were waving awkwardly, as you would expect a newborn to; its skin was a color I had never seen before. Jesus shifted the baby to one hand for a moment, as He extended His other hand out in a sweeping wave and said to me, "For **all** these, I died." With that strong statement, He raised the baby upward in both hands, high before the cross.

In that incredible moment, I received instant revelation that the color of the baby, a color not seen before, represented the blend of all races. You see, it doesn't matter your color or background; whether you are male or female, rich or poor, young or old, if you have influence or no one—He died to save you. To bring **you** back into right-standing with the Father, for all have sinned and are in need a Savior— His Name is Jesus.

Just as suddenly as I left, I became aware that I was again present in the room, as if just awakening. The song that had started when the vision began, was just coming to an end. In the time of a single song, I was shown the simple but profound message that Jesus came into the world, as a baby Himself, to tell. In each incident I had witnessed the people, in their own culture, carrying on the activities of their life. We are all unique and we carry the tradition we are raised in, but before Jesus, we blend as ONE. We are one nation and one color in His eyes— the color of Love!

"And Peter opened his mouth and said: 'Truly I perceive that God shows no partiality, but in every nation any one who fears him and does what is right is acceptable to him.'" Acts 10:34

"After this I looked, and behold, a great multitude which no man could number, from every nation, from all tribes and peoples and tongues, standing before the throne and before the Lamb, clothed in white robes, with palm branches in their hands, and crying out with a loud voice, 'Salvation belongs to our God who sits upon the throne, and to the Lamb!'" Revelation 7:9-10

Measured Within

The true measure of a man—his stature—is measured from within. The appearance may not always be true to you, but I see within and *therein are no lies*.

I know **fully** the make-up of a man, for the part that you cannot see is the heart—*the heart I see*.

You judge appearances—how can that be?

How can you judge what you cannot see?

Yes, the fruit will tell—what falls from the tree. Yet, still you've no right to judge, *for judgement is not for thee*. Do you know where he's been, what has happened before then? Do you know his dreams or failures from when?

When you know all that I know, then you shall judge.

Will that ever be?

No, you'd best leave him to Me. That is My plea—

Just leave him to Me!

"Judge not, that you be not judged. For with the judgment you pronounce you will be judged, and the measure you give will be the measure you get. Why do you see the speck that is in your brother's eye, but don't notice the log that is in your own eye?" Matthew 7:1-3

"Let all bitterness and wrath and anger and clamor and slander be put away from you, with all malice, and be kind to one another, tenderhearted, forgiving one another, as God in Christ forgave you." Ephesians 4:31-32

"There is one lawgiver and judge, he who is able to save and to destroy. But who are you that you judge your neighbor?" James 4:12

The Path You Choose to See

Do you see that there are two paths, and yet it is one and the same—the path that you see?

Many see it as a fork in the road, and they have a choice, a decision to make. But, in reality, it is one path. Your choices determine your direction, but it is one path. It leads to life, it leads to death, depending on which way you face—the choice you make, the steps you place.

Do you see then, that moving forward only comes from being consistent in your choices? For if you are contrary, you turn away—you head that way.

The double-minded man spends his life in the same spot; continually turning, neither advancing nor retreating, he digs a hole right where he is. (James 1:5-8)

All are encompassed by the life they choose.

One might say, 'I am accountable to no one' for **they** are the maker of the life '**they** lead.' Yet, when they die, many look to Me to blame, as if I had failed—as if I could be untrue. (Proverbs 14:12-14)

Man builds his life by the choices he makes; by the words he speaks, by the actions he takes. (Proverbs 18:21)

Even the food he eats is a choice. It will nourish the body and cause it to thrive or deplete the very life he's been given.

- ❖ Choose life or choose death.
- ❖ Build up or tear down.
- ❖ Walk forward or stand still.

Blessing or cursing—you choose!

Choose Life!

For every effect, there is a cause. One tries to figure out—why? And would conclude—be**cause** this.

For every cause will be.

Think about what you will cause to be.

Choose life!

Choose what you want to be.

"Listen to advice and accept instruction, that you may gain wisdom for the future." Proverbs 19:20

"Give instruction to a wise man, and he will be still wiser; teach a righteous man and he will increase in learning. The fear of the Lord is the beginning of wisdom, and the knowledge of the Holy One is insight. For by me your days will be multiplied, and years will be added to your life." Proverbs 9:9-11

Be Right or Be Left

Are you right or left-handed? You are born with natural tendencies and some are stronger than others, but you will develop what you practice; most will choose to favor one over the other.

Are you left or right?

So, you are born with a spirit nature—that you develop by your choices. Do you favor left or right? You are not forced into a mold. Even a child, when influenced, must make his own decision and will grow to live by the decisions he makes.

Child's play develops—adult decisions envelop—all must choose.

Right or left—right or wrong, decisions all lifelong. Some merely hinder, but some will never escape from the choices they've made. In stubbornness, they cling to the way that seems right, but the end therein is destruction. (Proverbs 16:25)

Are you right or left-handed?

It matters not.

But right and wrong is a matter of the heart.

You choose to develop, what will envelop you.

Choose rightly—choose life!

"I call heaven and earth to witness against you this day, that I have set before you life and death, blessing and curse; therefore choose life, that you and your decedents may live, loving the Lord your God, obeying his voice, and cleaving to him; for that means life to you and length of days—" Deuteronomy 30:19-20a

"Who is the man that fears the Lord? Him will he instruct in the way that he should choose. He himself will abide in prosperity, and his children shall possess the land. The friendship of the Lord is for those who fear him, and he makes known to them his covenant. My eyes are ever toward the Lord, for he will pluck my feet out of the net." Psalms 25:12-15

"For a man's ways are before the eyes of the Lord, and he watches all his paths. The iniquities of the wicked ensnare him, and he is caught in the toils of his sin. He dies for lack of discipline, and because of his great folly he is lost." Proverbs 5:21-23

"When the Son of man comes in his glory, and all the angels with him, then he will sit on his glorious throne. Before him will be gathered all the nations, and he will separate them one from another as a shepherd separates the sheep from the goats, and he will place the sheep at his right hand, but the goats at the left." Matthew 25:31-33

I'M Calling

It appears that the days are getting shorter and that time is speeding up. There is an urgency in the air and I want you to recognize that time is indeed running out.

Sin is rampant and many have grown cold—even to their family members. There are many who once believed My Word, but have begun to wane; for they believe that I have taken too long in 'making good' My Promises, especially My Promise to return. (Micah 7:6-7)

Is it too long, My friend, if another day would save a soul from Hell? If you had to choose from your friends and loved ones, which one would you discard?

Exactly!

There isn't one of you that I would choose to let go of either. It is My desire that all will come to the knowledge of the Truth—that all will be saved.

The heart-breaking truth is that all will not be—even though they can be. Just as in the days of Noah, many refuse to believe. They call it a fairy tale and laugh in My Face; in much the same way the guards spit in My Face.

Oh, but I love them, and beseech the Father to wait!

For it just may be **your** friend I'm waiting for.

Or

It just may be **you**.

Don't wait or it may be too late!

I'm Calling.

"And because wickedness is multiplied, most men's love will grow cold. But he who endures to the end will be saved." Matthew 24:12-13

"The Lord is not slow about his promise as some count slowness, but is forbearing toward you, not wishing that any should perish, but that all should reach repentance. But the day of the Lord will come like a thief, and then the heavens will pass away with a loud noise, and the elements will be dissolved with fire, and the earth and the works that are upon it will be burned up. Since all these things are thus to be dissolved, what sort of persons ought you to be in lives of holiness and godliness, waiting for and hastening the coming of the day of God, because of which the heavens will be kindled and dissolved, and the elements will melt with fire! But according to his promise we wait for new heavens and a new earth in which righteousness dwells. 'Therefore, beloved, since you wait for these, be zealous to be found by him without spot or blemish, and at peace. And count the forbearance of our Lord as salvation.'" II Peter 3:9-15a

~ I Timothy 2:1-6 ~ James 5:7-8 ~ Mark 13:35-36 ~

My Story

A captivating tale is a story that captures the heart. But, My Story, **is** the heart, the heart of the matter, and all that matters—for it is the beginning *and* the end. (Revelation 21:6-7 KJV)

Those who've thought they'd lost it all, can find new life in Me.

A new life is not a continuation of the old, it is new. Why then would you want to carry old thoughts into the new, as if they were unfinished business? Contemplating your past, as if it hadn't passed, holds your vision backward and hinders you from moving forward—a cause for stumbling.

Turn your face toward the Son!

Feel the warmth. I'm not behind you—I beckon you forward. Embrace this new life, as if the other never was. (John 12:26)

Manage your feelings, before they manage you!

"Therefore, if anyone is in Christ, he is a new creation; the old has passed away, behold, the new has come. All this is from God, who through Christ reconciled us to himself and gave us the ministry of reconciliation; that is, in Christ, God was reconciling the world to himself, not counting their trespasses against them, and entrusting to us the message of reconciliation. So we are ambassadors for Christ, God making his appeal through us. We beseech you on behalf of Christ, be reconciled to God. For our sake he made him to be sin who knew no sin, so that in him we might become the righteousness of God." II Corinthians 5:17-21

"—Jesus spoke to them, saying, 'I am the light of the world; he who follows me will not walk in darkness, but will have the light of life.'" John 8:12

"Jesus said to them, 'The light is with you for a little longer. Walk while you have the light, lest the darkness overtake you; he who walks in the darkness does not know where he goes. While you have the light, believe in the light, that you may become sons of light.'" John 12:35-36a

~ Psalms 36:7-9 ~ John 15:9-11 ~ Revelation 1:8 ~

Free of Nasty

Nice or Nasty? Both are behaviors of the heart; both seem common from the start. But things do not seem as though they do appear— for one behavior truly has its root planted in fear.

Fear can be complex; a given opportunity for the one who has lost trust to turn and heap fear upon thee. Nasty is a behavior of the heart of the one that carries wounds—hurts that run far and deep— troublesome even in their sleep, producing fruit that is nasty.

Do you know of one like this?

They toil and connive, their goal only to strive, against the one they see at peace—one who is nice and not nasty.

- ❖ My Love will heal their wounded heart.
- ❖ My Love will give them a brand-new start.
- ❖ My love will cause the soul to thrive, of the one who seems only to survive.

You who are nice ought to think twice about the one from whom you would rather run. For I call them dear, and ask you to lead them near— I wish to set them free from nasty.

Do you see?

Lord, could it be that this one is me? But for Your Love, there go I—

I was the one with a wounded heart, yet Your Love sustained . . .

- ❖ I lost trust, yet Your Love remained.
- ❖ I acted out, when others found peace.
- ❖ I the one seeking release, from nasty.

Oh Lord I see—that one is me!

Please, Father, hear my plea—to complete Your Love in me. There is an area, not yet free, from nasty; the room closed off—too painful to see; boarded and still—please take it from me. I've held on too long—it's grown much too strong. A place I can no longer trace—its root remains in me.

Please hear my plea!

My child, I have never left you. Yet, I needed for you to see, your whole heart you did not yield or give to Me—you've been holding back on Me. I can restore, will heal you completely, but it must begin with you; for I do not force Myself inside. Invite Me in to sup with thee; I will abide and you will thrive; as My Love reveals the pain, but only to wash away the stain, of the one who had lost their way.

I Love you!

You will be brand new when the work is through, but there yet remains one thing . . .

I cannot yet begin, or ever change, the one who **remains** the same. To begin, you must **admit** and then **submit** to the One who Loves you so. Let go of blame, and so refrain, from holding back—you **know**. I will complete the work in thee, with permission from you, that I might see—

all that you've held back—

Forever FREE,

if you would simply trust in Me!

"In a great house there are not only vessels of gold and silver but also of wood and earthenware, and some for noble use, some for ignoble. If anyone purifies himself from what is ignoble, then he will be a vessel for noble use, consecrated and useful to the master of the house, ready for any good work." II Timothy 2:20-21

"Strive for peace with all men, and for the holiness without which no one will see the Lord. See to it that no one fail to obtain the grace of God; that no "root of bitterness" spring up and cause trouble, and by it many become defiled." Hebrews 12:14-15

"—for God is at work in you, both to will and to work for his good pleasure." Philippians 2:13

"Not that I have already obtained this or am already perfect; but I press on to make it my own, because Christ Jesus has made me his own. Brethren, I do not consider that I have made it my own; but one thing I do, forgetting what lies behind and straining forward to what lies ahead, I press on toward the goal for the prize of the upward call of God in Christ Jesus. Let those of us who are mature be thus minded; and if in anything you are otherwise minded, God will reveal that also to you. Only let us hold true to what we have attained." Philippians 3:12-16

~ Luke 5:36-38 ~

A Real Life

The path of the sinner is unknown to him. He doesn't believe his destination, that of hell, therefore he 'knows' he is not headed there. So he 'tries' different pursuits, if they 'feel' right, and continues as long as no obstacle blocks his way—come what may. He is often a 'victim,' in dismay, of what 'life has dealt him'—many say. (Proverbs 16:25)

Child's play.

Are you ready for a real life?

One that holds plan and purpose? I know the beginning *and* the end. My plan for you to *see*, is where you enter in. (Matthew 7:13-14)

When we begin—you'll *see*!

It is so much more, your life I've prepared, than an escape from Hell. It was designed with you in mind, before the day you were born! (Psalms 139:16) (Jeremiah 1:5a)

You are My legacy—

the children I left behind, and I cherish each of you. A good man leaves an inheritance to his children's children—how much more have I left for you? (Proverbs 13:22) (Proverbs 20:7)

I had *you* in mind when I designed the end of all time—the legacy of My Life given; traced through My Blood, an endless genealogy; many like you, but they are not **you**. I had *you* in mind, from the beginning of time, with a purpose for only *you*!

You can waste life, choose to be left behind, or seek Me to see this plan through.

Come, see your life through My Eyes—see your life given.

For the One who gave, did not stay in the grave, **and neither should My plan for *you***!

"Seek the Lord while he may be found, call upon him while he is near; let the wicked forsake his way, and the unrighteous man his thoughts; let him return to the Lord, that he may have mercy on him, and to our God, for he will abundantly pardon. For my thoughts are not your thoughts, neither are your ways my ways, says the Lord." Isaiah 55:6-8

"Listen to advice and accept instruction, that you may gain wisdom for the future. Many are the plans in the mind of man, but it is the purpose of the Lord that will be established." Proverbs 19-20-21

"The Lord is my chosen portion and my cup; thou holdest my lot. The lines have fallen for me in pleasant places; yea, I have a goodly heritage. I bless the Lord who gives me counsel; in the night also my heart instructs me. I keep the Lord always before me; because he is at my right hand, I shall not be moved. Therefore my heart is glad, and my soul rejoices; my body also dwells secure. For thou dost not give me up to Sheol, or let thy godly one see the Pit. Thou dost show me the path of life; in thy presence there is fulness of joy, in thy right hand are pleasures for evermore." Psalms 16:5-11

Fire Burns Within

The dimly burning wick shall not be quenched!

I have seen your sorrows and witnessed your sadness, yet you have not turned away. Your heart is not cold. You cling to what was, but that is no longer you— you have grown. Trials and hardships have matured you, strengthened what was weak.

Yet, all you see is ash, too weary to speak.

Stir up the coals, for fire burns within. All is not lost, there is forgiveness for your sin. (Psalms 32:2-5)

Stir up the gifts, fan the flame.

Reclaim your life—there's more to gain.

Ask of Me and I'll give you the nations; restore prayer, rebuke indignation.

YOU ARE STILL MINE, and there is much to do. Stir up the fire—*still within you.*

Yes, time is getting short, but it's not over yet. Get off your bed of sorrow. It's time we were moving on, there's so much more for you to do.

So much more for you!

"—I remind you to rekindle the gift of God that is within you through the laying on of my hands; for God did not give us a spirit of timidity but a spirit of power and love and self-control." II Timothy 1:6

"Ask of me, and I will make the nations your heritage, and the ends of the earth your possession." Psalms 2:8

Stand for Truth

The world will allure those who are not standing for My Truth.

For if you are not standing, then you are falling—

it is as simple as that.

So many think this is not so, they laugh and think that their way is ok. But, let Me repeat, if you are not standing for My Truth, you are falling. Your loss is far greater than you can imagine. In terms of what could be yours, and the terror that remains, if you choose not to stand for My Truth.

"Good and upright is the Lord; therefore, he instructs sinners in the way." Psalms 25:8

As a child, did you imagine life as a princess or king?

That is what My Truth can bring. Were there bad dreams of your running in fear? That's in store for all who fall.

Can you tell Me why you would choose the latter? Live as a king or fear it will bring; for those who refuse—you'll lose . . .

For all must choose—there is no 'other' way.

"Do not love the world or the things in the world. If anyone loves the world, love for the Father is not in him. For all that is in the world, the lust of the flesh and the lust of the eyes and the pride of life, is not of the Father but is of the world. And the world passes away, and the lust of it; but he who does the will of God abides forever." I John 2:15-17

"For God has not destined us for wrath, but to obtain salvation through our Lord Jesus Christ, who died for us so that whether we wake or sleep we might live with him." I Thessalonians 5:9-10

"Therefore, brethren, be the more zealous to confirm your call and election, for if you do this you will never fall; so there will be richly provided for you an entrance into the eternal kingdom of our Lord and Savior Jesus Christ." II Peter 1:10-11

"Who is the man that fears the Lord? Him will he instruct in the way that he should choose. He himself shall abide in prosperity, and his children shall possess the land. The friendship of the Lord is for those who fear him, and he makes known to them his covenant. My eyes are ever toward the Lord, for he will pluck my feet out of the net." Psalms 25:12-15

~ Hebrews 12:25-29 ~ II Corinthians 5:10 ~ Psalms 37:9-11 ~

Final Question

Apostasy, apathy, indifference, anger, hunger, pain, loss—need I go on?

Emotions are stretched, hearts are hurting. The soul has lost control, for it was never meant to *be* in control.

Would you have your emotions run your life?

Many do, and then wonder why their life is out of control. I created you spirit, soul, and body. You are a human being, created in My image. (Genesis 1:26-27)

If I were to rule from emotion, of which would you prefer I rule?

- ❖ Anger or Compassion?
- ❖ Judgment or Forgiveness?

I am all of these and more—I AM Love.

I ruled with Love when I gave My Son to take your place—

that is My Grace—that is My Love.

"For God so loved the world that he gave his only Son, that whoever believes in him should not perish but have eternal life. For God sent the Son into the world, not to condemn the world, but that the world might be saved through him. He who believes in him is not condemned; he who does not believe is condemned already, because he has not believed in the name of the only Son of God." John 3:16-18

You think through emotion and focus on sin. You find someone that you think has greater sin than you and point fingers—lay blame. Defensive strategy to take the focus off you, and the question. You see, it is the 'question' I look to for each individual—their answer determines their fate.

Answer, before it's too late!

I don't look to sin, the type doesn't matter, for all have sinned as you know. What I look to is your **decision**—the answer to My question—*this is your judgement call.* (John 3:19-21)

Have you received My Son as your Lord and Savior—received His Blood for your sin?

He lived and died that you may abide, forever, as if you'd not sinned.

Now, if you have, then one emotion should be overwhelming—that of joy—for you are welcomed into My Kingdom, where Love rules! (Isaiah 12:3)

Judgement must fall upon all, but all are welcome to receive the Blessing of My Son, Jesus Christ. To all who **believe**, I call you son—*for all eternity.*

"—For there is no distinction; since all have sinned and fall short of the glory of God, they are justified by his grace as a gift, through the redemption which is in Christ Jesus, whom God put forward as an expiation by his blood, to be received by faith. This was to show God's righteousness, because in his divine forbearance he has passed over former sins; it was to prove at the present time that he himself is righteous and that he justifies him who has faith in Jesus." Romans 3:22b-26

~ Psalms 49:7-15 ~ I Thessalonians 5:9-10 ~ II Peter 1:10-11 ~
~ I Corinthians 15:19-22 ~

A Glorious Entrance
A True Testimony

My relationship with the Lord began when I was around nine years old. We talked back and forth all the time, but I never gave it much thought; it just seemed natural to me. Then it was in my early twenties that I developed a deep hunger to know more of Him.

One day, while resting on my bed, Jesus entered my room. The room so filled with the Glory of the Lord that I could not look up. In an audible voice, He said to me, "Ask Me into your heart." "I've already done that." I responded. His reply was simply, "Ask Me again." "Lord Jesus, please come into my heart." It was a simple prayer. At that, a great weight pressed down upon me; it seemed only seconds or a maybe a minute. Then the weight lifted and the brilliance of His Glory was gone. I remember running to the mirror to see if I looked different, recalling that Moses' face had shone when he came away from the Presence of the Lord. I don't know if I looked different, but I certainly was—my life was never to be the same again.

That life-changing moment preceded a series of steps to introduce me to the Baptism of the Holy Spirit. Finally, my heart, that for years had been crying out for more, was satisfied. The Bible opened up to me with new understanding. My faith grew, amazing answers to prayer and miracles were happening to me at every turn.

I had a heart that hungered for Him, but there were many years that I was not living a Christian lifestyle. Salvation without the Word is a car without gas, going nowhere, as one of His messages has taught me. The soul remains unchanged, mind not renewed. Yes, the Blood saves us, if only we confess our sin, ask and believe, but that is just the beginning. To be transformed, into the image of the Son, we must continually feed and be washed in the Word. He gave me a fresh new start; it didn't change my salvation—it changed me!

My Delight

I took delight on the day My Son was bruised. Not because it pleased Me to see Him abused, broken, but that His meek obedience satisfied the payment required for you to be grafted in. A price so high could only be paid by the pure sacrifice of Holiness, the shed Blood of a sinless Man.

It satisfied Me.

You are that important to Me!

Do you stop and consider that? Really **own** it in your heart, how very valuable and priceless you are to Me; that I could watch My one and only Son be—

brutally beaten,

spit upon,

tortured,

hung and left to die,

nails run through His hands and feet.

One born for victory, but never defeat!

How precious is your life, that He gave His own life, that you'd be made free!

You have only to *believe,* in order to *receive* that priceless Blood—no greater value has been found.

No greater love been given—

than the day I turned My Face from My Son.

My prize was you—to be won!

I saw My Son, so priceless—

but, for a moment, turned away.

Looking back I saw you—

through the Blood, I saw you!

I took delight on the day that My Son was bruised—

and that delight, My child, was YOU!

"—he has appeared once for all at the end of the age to put away sin by the sacrifice of himself. And just as it is appointed for men to die once, and after that comes judgment, so Christ, having been offered once to bear the sins of many, will appear a second time, not to deal with sin but to save those who are eagerly waiting for him." Hebrews 9:26b-28

~ Isaiah 53:3-12 ~

The Journey
A True Testimony

"Come on a journey with Me," Jesus whispered to my heart. I lay on the floor, face down, with arms stretched out in front; expressing my heart of surrender, in reverence, to the Lord of my life. He has brought me through so much—so much more than saving my life, He has given me life.

The vision began with Christ's experience of the cross. From the first nail to the hand, it continued on, as I was given a *taste* of the pain and agony that He had experienced. There is no way I could know the true horror of the pain, that would be more than anyone could bear; just this example had left my spirit writhing and shaking in anguish.

In the vision, various parts of His body were introduced, as if magnified. I witnessed, as if first-hand, His Blood-oozing face where chunks of flesh were missing; His beard having been literally ripped out of His skin. Blood running down His forehead where thorns pierced His skin. I felt pressure in my feet as if pressing down against the metal stake run through. My neck felt the stretch and pain as I watched His head loll against His chest—His body no longer offered strength to hold His head upright.

In utter sadness I realized that I had hung Jesus there. My sin joined that of all mankind, for I was no better—no one is.

Sin is sin to the Lord, all separate man from the Father, all had to be paid for. To reinstate relationship of God to man, Jesus paid the ultimate price for me—for you. I cried out in my heart. "Oh, Lord Jesus forgive me, please, forgive me." I know well, His forgiveness, but suddenly there was such a need to express what was churning in my heart, no other words but repentance. How can anyone not receive such an unselfish and heroic sacrifice? How can anyone be indifferent to such a horrific price paid for their soul?

When I thought I could bear no more, the vision directed me to a Centurion soldier. He stood with sword in hand, staring at it as if in disbelief; sun glinting off shiny steel, but a third of the sword, toward the tip, was not shiny but coated in thick, dark red blood. He held it with tip pointed toward the ground and stood with a look of shock on his face, as if in realization of what he had done. I believe this was the sword that had pierced Jesus' side, drawn Blood from the Savior of the world—Blood shed for you and for me.

This arduous journey continued, revealing a sepulcher; somewhat rounded in shape but completely gray, an almost shapeless mound; somewhat familiar, like what a child might form out of a lump of clay. This appeared to be a gravesite, located in an open field, desolate. Three fences made of rustic jagged lengths of wood extended out from a beginning point at the gravesite.

A light skiff of snow on the ground responded to a bitter, wicked wind that blew sharp, swirl-like gusts of fine, dry, snow against the tomb. The grave in the midst of this barren field appeared to be empty, gray, lifeless. Staring at this tomb for a seemingly endless time, with great sadness in my heart, no thoughts came as I looked at this lonely grave. But simply experiencing the powerful feeling of cold emptiness—incredibly exhausted, and wondering when it would end.

Noticing a path that led away from the grave, I followed it, leaving the field behind. The fences were no longer visible as I walked away. This stretch was sparsely tree-lined and consisted of about 4-6 inches of sand above hard-packed earth; enough to make walking very difficult, as my feet dredged through it. The trees and sand were all the same color, sort of a dark tan. This mundane and bland expanse seemed to match the overwhelming sadness in my heart; no other color was available until I reached the very end of my exhausting trek.

To my right, at a distance, I could see a lake of a beautiful shade of blue. On it were sailboats, with colorfully striped sails. It appeared to be a warm and sunny day, a happy day, as I heard faint laughter ringing out from far away. I love water, so this would normally be very appealing to me; but on this day I felt indifferent to it, as if it held no relevance to me or my life. I was weary from my long trudge through the sand and felt no tangible emotion toward the beauty that I could see—as if nothing really mattered anymore. The path ended right in front of me, as if there was nothing beyond.

Standing there, feeling almost shapeless myself, it seemed as if I was living a theme of suffering. There have been continuous times of spiritual growth, but again and again the path returns to the journey of sand, the path of suffering. As I stood there taking this in, only one thought came to mind and with great effort I expressed it. "What now Lord, how do I get beyond this?"

Our lives are carved and shaped by experiences we encounter. In the midst of trial, I have experienced many wonderful miracles that always make me hunger for more, and encourage me to strive to break free from the past. Nothing I have ever faced has dimmed those wonderful blessings—the gifts that have called me forward, kept me going; convincing me that there is a higher calling to fulfill—something yet to come.

It is in 'the journey' that we come to know God; and in suffering we learn who we are, what we yet need to be, and where we are going. It is our plumb line. The grave was the beginning, rather than the end. We leave the shapeless mound of death, that of our past, to be shaped for our future—it is a journey.

As I was experiencing the vision of the journey, someone else in the room had a vision as well. He spoke of a woman kneeling in a canoe, her arms raised in surrender, as the canoe carried her along a river that opened into a lake.

As if his vision was the answer to my question—kneel, surrender, worship—these steps begin the journey, in guiding one to their **true** destiny.

.

You Are Priceless

You estimate the value of your life by studying the circumstances that you live in. If those circumstances improve, then you deem that you are more valuable—as if your actions could increase your worth.

I call you Mine!

Set apart from the world.

Redeemed.

Bought with My Blood.

No other human being was ever sinless, and yet bore the sin of the world. No higher price could be paid. I did this for you! Do you then, think that you are not valuable to Me? Can you improve your worth?

- ❖ You are priceless!
- ❖ Nothing you can name has more value.
- ❖ Nothing calls My attention like you do.

Spend time with Me.

Value Me, like I value you.

"For what can a man give in return for his life?" Mark 8:37

"Look at the birds of the air: they neither sow nor reap nor gather into barns, and yet your heavenly Father feeds them. Are you not of more value than they?" Matthew 6:26

"But now in Christ Jesus you who once were far off have been brought near in the blood of Christ." Ephesians 2:13

"He who has my commandments and keeps them, he It is who loves me; and he who loves me will be loved by my Father, and I will love him and manifest myself to him." John 14:21

"But when the time had fully come, God sent forth his Son, born of woman, born under the law, to redeem those who were under the law, so that we might receive adoption as sons. And because you are sons, God has sent the Spirit of his Son into our hearts, crying, "Abba! Father!" So through God you are no longer a slave but a son, and if a son then an heir." Galatians 4:4-7

~ Galatians 2:20 ~ Isaiah 43:4 ~

Date Nights with Jesus
A True Testimony

There was a time in my life when I struggled with darkness. Depression had settled upon me like a dense covering that was choking the life out of me. I cried myself to sleep many nights, and found myself crying even harder when I woke up to realize that I had not died in my sleep. I didn't understand, at the time, that this is a death wish that needs to be repented of, for it presents an open door for the devil to torment further.

Depression is very real—a soul out of control. My emotions had taken over and I had become a slave to my mind. I know now that, had I built my spirit, my inner man, to be strong in the Word, I would have been armored with the tools to stand strong against the enemy trying to take my life.

Years ago, I had faced a dark presence, whether the devil or a demon, I do not know, he didn't introduce himself. What I know is that I had come home so tired from work that I fell into bed with my uniform on and fell fast asleep with the light still on. I was rudely awakened sometime in the night, by a man dressed well in an all-black suit. His image void of light, but transparent, in that I could see through. If you are familiar with graphics, it was as if an opaque image is made more transparent by adjusting saturation.

This figure reached out his arms, attempting to strangle me. I struggled as his long arms wrapped both my upper body and around my face, blocking my mouth. I fought hard inside, knowing that if I could speak the Name of Jesus, this demonic form would be forced to flee. I fought hard to get that Name out and at the same time was struggling to breathe.

Finally, JESUS, burst forth from my mouth. I had spoken the Name and instantly his arms were off me. But before departing, he viciously declared, "I'll get you yet!" "Oh no you won't!" came my immediate retort, and with that, he vanished.

Just then, I looked up at the door of my room and was struck with what I saw. It had been there all along, but in revelation my eyes opened to it, as if seeing it for the first time. There hanging on the door was a tapestry that was sent to me from a friend. It was a colorfully-worked, full-sized image of a participant of cultural festivities from another land; a costumed person that looked like a devil. Immediately my eyes were opened to the darkness invited in; an open door to the occult and demonic forces, yet it had seemed a harmless gift.

I got up immediately, yanked the tapestry down, rolled it up and drove it to a dumpster; holding it out the window of my car. Back home, praying out loud, I took authority over my home and was never visited in that way again.

This present battle was a different form of darkness; a darkness clouding a hurting soul. Again, Jesus came to my rescue. When I awakened from the first dream, I remember trying hard to go back to sleep.

Great was the Love I had experienced. I was caught away with Jesus and I will never forget His eyes. The depth was so great, it was as if you could get lost in them. So all-encompassing was His Love, that He made me feel precious and priceless. No human can give such love—complete Love. The date nights became a pattern that lasted for six weeks, once a week, and sustained me through the darkness— healing my heart to cope again. It is a time I will never forget. He truly is the Lover and Savior of my soul.

Is There Room for Me?

My birth was not a 'season' but the beginning of the end—which is the beginning.

All must die, for the body is not eternal. The spirit would live forever were it not for sin. Sin brought death to the spirit, while the body lived on—for the spirit to live for eternity it must be born anew—made new.

"—Jesus answered him, 'Truly, truly, I say to you, unless one is born anew, he cannot see the kingdom of God.'" John 3:3

Renew

I came as a child that you might *see*.

I came as a babe that you might believe . . .

that you could be made new—totally freed, from a life of sin and death. A life without Me—yearns to be *free*.

Invite Me to your home this night. Ask Me in—I'll bring the light. Then you'll *see* that all you need is the gift that was given—the One True Light. (John 1:4, 9)

That Light is Me.

There was no room at the Inn, *will you ask Me in?*

"And the angel said to her, 'Do not be afraid, Mary, for you have found favor with God. And behold, you will conceive in your womb and bear a son, and you shall call his name Jesus. He will be great, and will be called the Son of the Most High; and the Lord God will give to him the throne of his father David, and he will reign over the house of Jacob forever; and of his kingdom there will be no end.'" Luke 1:30-33

"And she gave birth to her first-born son and wrapped him in swaddling clothes, and laid him in a manger, because there was no place for them in the inn." Luke 2:7

"But to all who received him, who believed in his name, he gave power to become children of God; who were born, not of blood nor of the will of the flesh nor of the will of man, but of God. And the Word became flesh and dwelt among us, full of grace and truth; we have beheld his glory, glory as of the only Son from the Father." John 1:12-14

"For the wages of sin is death, but the free gift of God is eternal life in Christ Jesus our Lord." Romans 6:23

The Key and More

It is good that you *wait* for My Voice. There are many voices in this world, clamoring for your attention; some would seem to have good intentions and some, it is evident, do not. (I Timothy 4:7-8)

"—the sheep hear his voice, and he calls his own sheep by name and leads them out. When he has brought out all his own, he goes before them, and the sheep follow him, for they know his voice. A stranger they will not follow, but they will flee from him, for they do not know the voice of strangers." John 10:3-5

Listen

Do not be hasty to obey—if you are unsure of the call, *wait*. (Philippians 2:12-13)

I AM in no hurry and neither should you be. I take you slowly, but steadily forward; sure, strong steps that you not slip and therefore become discouraged.

Practice is essential, with each new task—you learn.

Do not be hasty to arrive, but think about your stride. My direction is all around you, when you seek inside; confusion will never lead you.

Stop, listen.

Do nothing more than run to the door.

Open the door to Me, that you may see, but do not run out the door without your keys.

Do you see?

I will be your guide, but you must wait on Me. I AM the key that unlocks the door to more.

I AM the Door.

"So Jesus again said to them, 'Truly, truly, I say to you, I am the door of the sheep. All who came before me are thieves and robbers; but the sheep did not heed them. I am the door; if any one enters by me, he will be saved, and will go in and out and find pasture. The thief comes only to steal and kill and destroy; I came that they may have life, and have it abundantly.'" John10:7-10

I AM More.

"I am the good shepherd; I know my own and my own know me, as the Father knows me and I know the Father; and I lay my life down for the sheep." John 10:14-15

I AM

"Jesus said to them, 'Truly, truly, I say to you, before Abraham was, I am.'" John 8:58

Key

"He who conquers shall be clad thus in white garments, and I will not blot his name out of the book of life; I will confess his name before my Father and before his angels. He who has an ear, let him hear what the Spirit says to the churches." "And the angel of the church in Philadelphia write: 'The words of the holy one, the true one, who has the key of David, who opens and no one shall shut, who shuts and no one opens.'" Revelation 3:5-7

Now Listen.

"My sheep hear my voice, and I know them, and they follow me; and I give them eternal life, and they shall never perish, and no one shall snatch them out of my hand." John 10:27-28

"Behold, I stand at the door and knock; if anyone hears my voice and opens the door, I will come in to him and eat with him, and he with me. He who conquers, I will grant him to sit with me on my throne, as

I myself conquered and sat down with my Father on his throne. He who has an ear, let him hear what the Spirit says to the churches." Revelation 3:20-22

~ Colossians 1:9-14 ~

Take a Bow

Admission is the first step of action to be saved. You must admit to yourself, and then to Me, that you have sinned and you need a Savior. It takes great courage to become humble. It takes great humility to become saved.

The Children of Israel were a stiff-necked people, unyielding and refusing to bow. It cost them the promised land and many, their lives. (Numbers 14:21-24)

You may take a lesson, on what not to do, by reading the accounts of My children from long-past. The names have been recorded as a statement to the world that stubborn rebellion is a costly game to play, with stakes too high, the outcome sure death.

Whereas, true humility begins with death but the outcome is Life Eternal. (II Chronicles 30:8-9)

The bill marked Paid in Full!

Learn to bow before Me.

- ❖ The first time comes the hardest—you feel shy, embarrassed, unsure.
- ❖ The second time, you've stumbled—you're defensive, nervous.
- ❖ Third—you're broken, ashamed.

With every bow you are more clear of that need of a Savior.

With every bow—that need.

With every bow—more freed.

Bow before Me in **true** humility. With every bow—

True kneed

"God opposes the proud, but gives grace to the humble." "Humble yourselves before the Lord and he will exalt you." James 4:6b, 10

"For we shall all stand before the judgment seat of God; for it is written, "As I live, says the Lord, every knee shall bow to me, and every tongue shall give praise to God." So each of us shall give account of himself to God." Romans 14:10b-12

"The reward for humility and fear of the Lord is riches and honor and life." Proverbs 22:4

~ Psalms 51:1-4 ~

The Whole Measure

Measure by measure your faith is made whole. You have been given a measure of faith and, yes, it can move a mountain, but faith comes by hearing and hearing increases your measure. (Matthew 17:20-21)

Measure by measure, the more you hear, the more it becomes clear. The more you draw near, the more measure will be given.

Wholeness—A complete picture.

Wholeness—A deeper understanding.

Measure by measure a heart will mend, when given a full measure, as one learns to depend—

on the One who gave it all!

If good measure, shaken together and running over, shall be given to you by men when you give—

How much more?

How much more!

When you give your ear to Me.

"Give, and it shall be given unto you; good measure, pressed down, and shaken together, and running over, shall men give into your bosom. For with the same measure that ye mete withal it shall be measured to you again." St. Luke 6:38 KJV

"And Jesus answered them, 'Truly, I say to you, if you have faith and never doubt, you will not only do what has been done to the fig tree, but even if you say to this mountain, Be taken up and cast into the sea, it will be done. And whatever you ask in prayer, you will receive, if you have faith.'" Matthew 21:21-22

"And he said to them, 'Take heed what you hear; the measure you give will be the measure you get, and still more will be given you. For to him who has will more be given; and from him who has not, even what he has will be taken away.'" Mark 4:24-25

~ Isaiah 55:2-3, 10-11 ~ Matthew 13:23 ~

Built to Last

You've been beaten down, but you're not beaten!

Remember that!

Tear down all the things in your life that do not seem right, but don't give up on the fight.

When it seems as though your life is a confusing mess—a mass of confusion—tear down until you reach Truth—Rock solid.

If what is built isn't right, tear down until it is and build again.

Just build again.

Build from the Truth that you know, judge your life as you go, but don't stop building. Reconstruction is part of life—all must take time to fix what's not right.

Begin again . . .

and again.

It may seem then that you're not getting anywhere, but it is one life. With each re-build, you have—

- ❖ More wisdom.
- ❖ More knowledge and understanding.
- ❖ Your contracting skills are improved—increased.
- ❖ Lesson learned—more is released.

The final building—without blemish.

Matured to stand the storm—less mess.

Don't shy new construction—tear it down, to build you up!

Built to stand—

Built to last!

"For we are God's fellow workers; you are God's field, God's building.
According to the grace of God given to me, like a skilled master builder
I laid a foundation, and another man is building upon it. Let each man
take care how he builds upon it. For no other foundation can any one
lay than that which is laid, which is Jesus Christ. Now if any one builds
on the foundation with gold, silver, precious stones, wood, hay,
straw`—each man's work will become manifest; for the Day will
disclose it, because it will be revealed with fire, and the fire will test
what sort of work each one has done. If the work which any man has
built on the foundation survives, he will receive a reward. If any man's
work is burned up, he will suffer loss, though he himself will be saved,
but only as through fire." I Corinthians 3:9-15

~ II Peter 3:9-14 ~

A Clean Page

See your life each morning as a fresh new page.

You are not starting a new book or chapter, but you are adding to what has been written.

"Let me hear in the morning of thy steadfast love, for in thee I put my trust. Teach me the way I should go, for to thee I lift up my soul." Psalms 143:8

Most memories you will not be able to crumple and discard as you would a miswritten page. No, you carry them throughout your life, but they serve to improve, enhance, and even motivate you as you walk the path.

What has caused you to stumble will remind you to not walk that way again. Pass on by the hurtful entries—you must not reread them. They can control you, if you let them; but I remind you that My Blood is sufficient and complete—you lack nothing!

You are made perfect by My righteousness.

The price has been paid for every painful, hurtful event in your life. I carried you, by first carrying it to the cross.

Be satisfied knowing you have no loss!

You are complete in Me.

So, when memories come to taunt, say—'It's under the Blood—you will hurt me no more!'

I am the Beloved.

I am Loved!

"But when Christ had offered for all time a single sacrifice for sins, he sat down at the right hand of God, then to wait until his enemies should be made a stool for his feet. For by a single offering he has perfected for all time those who are sanctified." Hebrews 10:12-14

"And you, who were dead in trespasses and the uncircumcision of your flesh, God made alive together with him, having forgiven us all our trespasses, having cancelled the bond which stood against us with its legal demands; this he set aside, nailing it to the cross. He disarmed the principalities and powers and made a public example of them, triumphing over them in him." Colossians 2:13-15

"To him who loves us and has freed us from our sins by his blood and made us a kingdom, priests to his God and Father, to him be glory and dominion for ever and ever. Amen." Revelation 1:5b-6

Active Duty

To open your heart to My messages means more than just reading or knowing; it means you agree, and do what you see and hear. If you are unclear, then ask for more direction. Be specific about what you don't know and I, in turn, will be specific in answering you.

We are a team, you and I.

But a team works together for a common goal—one that they have agreed upon or there is no team and the goal will never be reached.

Trust Me to forge a plan just for you.

I will be specific and I will guide you through. Before we begin, you must learn the basics. Just as a soldier is put through basic training before the battle, so I must train you.

- ❖ You are Equipped.
- ❖ You are Disciplined.
- ❖ You are Honored.

You Go!

When you go, you will be showing what you know and your now-trained ear will also hear. What may not be clear to others, will be to you.

- ❖ You will know when you need more Training.
- ❖ You will know when you need to Rest.
- ❖ You will know when you are Favored.

And you will know, as will all the rest—*when you are BLESSED!*

"And his gifts were that some should be apostles, some prophets, some evangelists, some pastors and teachers, to equip the saints for the work of the ministry, for building up the body of Christ, until we all attain to the unity of the faith and the knowledge of the Son of God, to mature manhood, to the measure of the stature of the fulness of Christ; so that we may no longer be children, tossed to and fro and carried about with every wind of doctrine, by the cunning of men, by their craftiness in deceitful wiles. Rather, speaking the truth in love, we are to grow up in every way unto him who is the head, into Christ, from whom the whole body, joined and knit together by every joint with which it is supplied, when each part is working properly, makes bodily growth and upbuilds itself in love." Ephesians 4:11-16

"You are my friends if you do what I command you. No longer do I call you servants, for the servant does not know what his master is doing; but I have called you friends, for all that I have heard from my Father I have made known to you. You did not choose me, but I chose you and appointed you that you should go and bear fruit and that your fruit should abide; so that whatever you ask the Father in my name, he may give it to you. This I command you, to love one another." John 15:14-17

~ II Corinthians 10:3-6 ~ Mark 4:14-20 ~ Isaiah 28:23-26 ~

Called to Fast
A True Testimony

One night I had a dream that was so clear, it was as a vision. I saw myself at a specific grocery store in town, pushing a big shopping cart in the produce section. In my dream, I heaped my cart full of many varieties of vegetables, and I saw myself cooking them and eating a big, heaping plateful.

Awakening with the realization that I was to follow through with the vision, I did just that. I had already eaten my first big plateful, when a cousin phoned that afternoon.

"My doctor has discovered a lump in my breast, and they suspect it may be cancer," she anxiously informed me. "I have to go in for a biopsy," she added, sounding clearly shaken. "God's got this!" I assured her. "He already has me fasting for you— I've already started!"

For the next two weeks, I ate nothing but a heaping plate of vegetables, morning and night and prayed for my cousin's condition. I was amazed at how good they tasted. It seemed so easy, but then when God calls the fast—He provides the anointing to do it.

My cousin called again to tell me she had felt an anointing, like fire, shoot through her breast.

At the end of the two weeks, she called to report that she had gone in for a biopsy. Her excitement was so great that her words were competing to be said. "They took sample after sample," she related. "They said, 'We don't know what's happened, but this isn't like any tissue we have ever seen before. This is not breast tissue or cancer— we don't know what this is.'"

They had taken so many samples, trying to figure it out, that there wasn't much of a lump left. She never had surgery and it never returned.

Isn't the Lord wonderful?

I so enjoyed eating those vegetables, that I continued the regimen but adding other things. My energy level increased so much from the vegetables that I desired more exercise. Over time, friends and family began commenting on my weight loss. It was amazing and wonderful to discover that in about six months, I had lost good deal of excess weight and hardly even noticed.

There are great rewards for obedience when there is joy in the journey!

There's No Better Way

The choice is yours, whether you walk the highway or travel the low path. Both lead to a destination, but is that destination your desired end?

You have a say in your future.

You had your way in salvation—I gave you room to grow. You'll have your day in judgment, should you not judge yourself by what you know. (I Corinthians 11:31-32)

Clarity of vision comes from walking in My Light; not ahead of it, nor behind, but My Light is cast upon you when you walk *with* Me. (Psalms 36:9)

So, if you choose to walk with Me, I choose the highway.

It is the *right* way, for those who *see*. The diligent choose the more difficult route, for it is easy to walk without a thought, stepping on those you find along the way. 'What does it matter?' 'For tomorrow's another day' . . .

It does matter to Me!

- ❖ Work on one thing—determine to love.
- ❖ Then take on the battle with your tongue.
- ❖ Judge no other, for I would have you to judge yourself.

Handle these three and more will be in store; but for now, work on this—it is key, for the greater walk is to 'love your neighbor as yourself.' There is no high way, no right way, no better way than this—

Love

"For you were called to freedom, brethren; only do not use your freedom as an opportunity for the flesh, but through love be servants of one another. For the whole law is fulfilled in one word, 'You shall love your neighbor as yourself.'" Galatians 5:13-14

"The way of the righteous is level; thou dost make smooth the path of the righteous. In the path of thy judgments, O Lord, we wait for thee; thy memorial name is the desire of our soul. My soul yearns for thee in the night, my spirit within me earnestly seeks thee. For when thy judgments are in the earth, the inhabitants of the world learn righteousness." Isaiah 26:7-9

"And a highway shall be there, and it shall be called the Holy Way; the unclean shall not pass over it, and fools shall not err therein. No lion shall be there, nor shall any ravenous beast come up on it; they shall not be found there, but the redeemed shall walk there. And the ransomed of the Lord shall return, and come to Zion with singing; everlasting joy shall be upon their heads; they shall obtain joy and gladness, and sorrow and sighing shall flee away." Isaiah 35:8-10

~ Romans 12:9-10 ~ I Peter 3:8-12 ~

The Right Choice

Blessing or circumstance?

You Choose.

Circumstances can change and vary throughout your life—sometimes good and others may be bad. But the Blessing is always good, constant, for those who purpose to do My Will.

"I delight to do thy will, O my God; thy law is within my heart." Psalms 40:8

I AM not a respecter of persons, in that all are welcome to get in the flow. All may desire My Blessing and I AM willing that all be Blessed, but My Blessing does not flow to all; for all do not choose the path that is good—the path of the righteous. (Acts 10:34-35)

Many scoff and banter at those who choose good, yet they long for the Blessings to flow in their life.

Very simple, change your ways.

For all are welcome and I welcome all.

My Love is boundless and My Blessing flows to all who will receive, if only you'd believe. (Proverbs 4:26-27)

"Thou meetest him that joyfully works righteousness, those that remember thee in thy ways." Isaiah 64:5a

Your scoffing is a brave front to hide the fear inside. I see clear to your heart of fear and long to comfort you. So I ask you, dear one, to set aside the bravado; relinquish your past, acknowledge your need, and I will not rest to see that you are BLESSED!

Take heed of My warning, the time is short and now is, that *you must choose*. (Isaiah 13:9)

Blessing or circumstances?

You Choose

"Blessed are those whose way is blameless, who walk in the law of the Lord! Blessed are those who keep his testimonies, who seek him with their whole heart, who also do no wrong, but walk in his ways!" Psalms 119:1-3

"Do not envy a man of violence and do not choose any of his ways; for the perverse man is an abomination to the Lord, but the upright are in his confidence. The Lord's curse is on the house of the wicked, but he blesses the abode of the righteous. Toward the scorners he is scornful, but to the humble he shows favor. The wise will inherit honor, but fools get disgrace." Proverbs 3:31-35

"I call heaven and earth to witness against you this day, that I have set before you life and death, blessing and curse; therefore choose life, that you and your descendants may live, loving the Lord your God, obeying his voice, and cleaving to him; for that means life to you and length of days, that you may dwell in the land which the Lord swore to your fathers, to Abraham, to Isaac, and to Jacob, to give them." Deuteronomy 30:19-20

~ Proverbs 2:6-8 ~ Psalms 128:1-2 ~

Did You Know?

Chains that bind are not benign, they are like cancer that continues to grow.

Think of what you know.

- ❖ You know that I have come to set you free.
- ❖ You know to put your faith and trust in Me.

So why are you not free?

You don't know . . .

You don't know the One who loves you so. (Colossians 2:6-7)

You don't 'know' Me or you would be free! (Galatians 5:1)

For bondage cannot remain in My Presence. Sickness has to flee when you cast your gaze upon Me.

Do you see?

Peter walked on water until he took his eyes off Me. Likewise, when you look away, you fail to see you are free. (Matthew 14:29-32)

Bondage grows when left to linger. You lack authority—given to set you free—

Speak it with Me!

I AM your Word—given for you to *command* your life as you grow. The power that's Mine, breaks chains that would bind—releasing you to go—

FREE!

I AM the Word.

Do you know Me?

"And the Word became flesh and dwelt among us, full of grace and truth; we have beheld his glory, glory as of the only Son from the Father." John 1:14

"Since then we have a great high priest who has passed through the heavens, Jesus, the Son of God, let us hold fast our confession. For we have not a high priest who is unable to sympathize with our weaknesses, but one who in every respect has been tempted as we are, yet without sin. Let us then with confidence draw near to the throne of grace, that we may receive mercy and find grace to help in time of need." Hebrews 4:14-16

"His divine power has granted to us all things that pertain to life and godliness, through the knowledge of him who called us to his own glory and excellence, by which he has granted to us his precious and very great promises, that through these you may escape from the corruption that is in the world because of passion, and become partakers of the divine nature." II Peter 1:3-4

~ Psalms 9:9-10 ~ Colossians 1:11-14 ~ Psalms 1:1-3 ~

A New Liver
A True Testimony

A white-faced and shaken co-worker related to me one day that she was scheduled to start the process for a liver transplant. An MRI had revealed that without a new liver, her life would soon come to an end. That message tore her heart, for she had a husband and young kids and anticipated a long life with them. I told her of God's healing power and related to her of healing stories that I had experienced.

She told me that she believed in God and was in agreement that God would heal her. I didn't lay hands on her, as often we Christians do. I kept searching my heart to see if He wanted me to, but didn't receive that lead. We were in agreement and believed.

One day at home, as I was praying for my co-worker, again the Lord spoke to my heart; so clear it seemed nearly audible but wasn't. "I have heard your prayer and I am going to heal her." As the tears streamed down my face, I rejoiced and thanked Him for His unending Faithfulness!

Over the period of about two weeks, the Lord asked me to relate to her a couple more stories of personal accounts I had experienced of His Healing Power, to build her faith, and keep her strengthened. She is amazing and grabbed ahold with a child-like faith that was matter of fact—a done deal. I am sure this made God smile. It wasn't begging or pleading or straining, just belief that what God says He will do—HE WILL.

"Again I say to you, if two of you agree on earth about anything they ask, it will be done for them by my Father in heaven. For where two

or three are gathered in my name, there am I in the midst of them."
Matthew 18:19-20

Unwavering Trust!

One time I did speak to her about fear. I could see something in her eyes. She admitted that she had some, well who wouldn't? But I explained that fear was the opposite of her goal, and it is double-minded. To be in faith—fear must go!

"Have no anxiety about anything, but in everything by prayer and supplication with thanksgiving let your requests be made known to God. And the peace of God, which passes all understanding, will keep your hearts and your minds in Christ Jesus." Philippians 4:6-7

Again, with that wonderful child-like trust, she cast fear down, firmed up her faith, and believed. In about a week and a half, she said she was feeling better. With a smile I said, "That's because you're healed!" she nodded in firm agreement. The hospital had called, but she was sleeping and they left a message. She tried to call them for a week but could only leave messages, that they didn't return. I told her that is because she is healed. She whole-heartedly agreed and at the end of two weeks, or thereabouts, went in for a second MRI.

Two MRI images were hung, side by side, and before them stood a puzzled doctor. Having no medical explanation for their difference, he questioned, "Why are you here? There's nothing wrong with you!" Her new MRI showed the same liver, but brand new, completely healed!

Praise Jesus—The Healer!

"O Lord my God I cried to thee for help, and thou hast healed me."
Psalms 30:2

Glory to God!

It wasn't my faith that brought forth her healing, it was hers! I had recently lost my husband to cancer, though I poured myself out for him to be healed and believed with all my heart. Healing is individual, and it is never God that fails. It is a connection of the heart in need with the Healing Power of God. Jesus is always willing to be your Healer. Healing power is always flowing out to you, if you simply believe. Doubt, fear, double-mindedness, words spoken in unbelief, all serve to quench the healing power of God. Fill your heart with the Word of God until it pushes out all unbelief, and out of a pure, believing heart flows the Words of Life.

If you are a born-again believer, it is your covenant right to walk in health. Your covenant says that you are already 'the healed' and sickness, disease the *trespasser*. Line up your heart, mind and especially your mouth with the Word of God. You need not beg God to heal; but as you pray to Him, standing on His word, simultaneously using your God-given *authority*, demand that sickness leave. Receive it as so, speak of your body healed. Many do not believe until they see the symptoms gone. Oh, if we would only believe **before** we see, then it **would** be! Find out what your covenant with God is and *live* in the fullness of all it contains.

Many say that God gives them sickness to teach them something. This is a lie from the enemy to keep you from receiving your promise from God. Embrace the Word of God and learn the Truth—it is the Truth that sets you free!

"He himself bore our sins in his body on the tree, that we might die to sin and live to righteousness. By his wounds you have been healed." I Peter 2:24

Jesus is the Healer.

He is always good! Don't believe a lie, but be built up in what His Word really says— to LIVE HEALED.

"—If you will diligently hearken to the voice of the Lord your God, and do that which is right in his eyes, and give heed to his commandments and keep all his statutes, I will put none of the diseases upon you which I put upon the Egyptians; for I am the Lord, your healer." Exodus 15:26

May we all attain the wonderful child-like faith that my co-worker displayed. May we all *receive* the gift of Healing that she received.

May we BELIEVE!

Scaling the Mountain

These times have been hard and I know you have struggled so. It has not been easy to watch you fight with each day, yet you must gain strength and know your weakness.

"I can do all things in him who strengthens me." Philippians 4:13

The higher climb is difficult terrain—scaling mountains you have only seen, from afar, in the past. Your enemy is nearer to your face when you are facing your mountain.

Speak to the mountain as you climb.

"Truly, I say to you, whoever says to this mountain, 'Be taken up and cast into the sea,' and does not doubt in his heart, but believes that what he says will come to pass, it will be done for him. Therefore, I tell you, whatever you ask in prayer, believe that you have received it, and it will be yours." Mark 11:23-24

With each new step, speak your accomplishment—speak your decisions. Do not look down to see how far you have come until you reach the top, for you will follow what you see.

Keep looking at Me!

The higher you climb, the clearer the view. You may understand when someone relates an experience to you, but when you climb that mountain yourself—you know!

Delight in accomplishment, celebrate the victory, but do not become prideful or you will fall. When pride comes to call, look around you at all you have yet to accomplish—look at Me—you're still small.

"Pride goes before destruction, and a haughty spirit before a fall." Proverbs 16:18

There is more to learn.

Always more!

But what I want you to know, as you're struggling so, you're not failing—you are continuing to grow. Fight the *good* fight of faith.

Use the tools you've been given.

You're nearer than you think; often it is only the top of the mountain that peaks out of the clouds. Climb until you reach the Glory and—

don't look back!

"Offer to God a sacrifice of thanksgiving, and pay your vows to the Most High; and call upon me in the day of trouble; I will deliver you and you shall glorify me." Psalms 50:14-15

"Now the Lord is the Spirit, and where the Spirit of the Lord is, there is freedom. And we all, with unveiled face, beholding the glory of the Lord, are being changed into his likeness from one degree of glory to another; for this comes from the Lord who is the Spirit." II Corinthians 3:17-18

"But thanks be to God, who in Christ always leads us to triumph, and through us spreads the fragrance of the knowledge of him everywhere." II Corinthians 2:14

"May the Lord give strength to his people! May the Lord bless his people with peace!" Psalms 29:11

~ Titus 2:7-8 ~ Titus 2:11-14 ~ Psalms 103:2-5 ~

The Secret to Success

Lessons often come hard and I would like to spare you that, and yet not.

For I know you will learn much from the difficulties you overcome; just as a parent watches his child struggle to accomplish a task, wants to stop and do it for him, but doesn't.

Love refrains from making life easy, but Love never leaves.

I AM always here to guide you.

You will overcome, accomplish, conquer, whichever word you prefer to describe that elation, I call victory!

My children are victorious, for I empower them.

David conquered Goliath, overcame the lion, the bear; yet from all appearance he was a boy—inside, a man of courage—a confident man. (I Samuel 17:36-37)

What was his secret?

That he practiced his slingshot?

He practiced worship!

In all his ways, he acknowledged Me. (Proverbs 3:6)

He worshipped.

He was built up on the inside, before the event, armored with My Power wherever he went.

Lions, bears, giants—no matter, I will see you through.

Worship Me intimately—The secret to success!

"Extol the Lord our God; worship at his footstool! Holy is he!" Psalms 99:5

"So David prevailed over the Philistine with a sling and with a stone, and struck the Philistine, and killed him; there was no sword in the hand of David." I Samuel 17:50

"O come, let us sing to the Lord; let us make a joyful noise to the rock of our salvation! Let us come into his presence with thanksgiving; let us make a joyful noise to him with songs of praise!" Psalms 95:1-2

"O come, let us worship and bow down, let us kneel before the Lord, our Maker! For he is our God, and we are the people of his pasture, and the sheep of his hand." Psalms 95:6-7

~ I Samuel 17:45-47 ~

Super-Naturally

Frustrations come when one attempts to 'work' with his *own* might. Man has been given strength to function in day-to-day tasks, but beyond daily living, the strength needed must come from above.

Supernatural strength is given, not earned.

Good works are the *fruit* of obedience but, unlike mans' ways, I do not award 'points' for being good. Every man begins a supernatural life by receiving My shed Blood. Your repentance releases your hold on the old; My Blood washes it all away—I never see it again and neither should you.

A relinquished life has no hold on you,

and you should no longer lay hold of it. Now, see what I see—

- ❖ A man that is brand new.
- ❖ Never has sinned.
- ❖ He has no faults.

Complete in every way—simply by My Blood.

So why would you need to earn points? No, rather, supernatural strength is given when the need for it arises. When you use what you have, more will be given; as you grow, so increases the requirement. Much like body building but this, My son, My daughter, is supernatural power!

You can fight a battle in the heavenlies without leaving your room—now that is power! That is only the beginning. The 'point' therefore, I AM making, is this—

Work with Me, not for Me.

If you are working **for** Me, you will earn wages for a job complete. Work **with** Me, and you as a son I treat. I will teach you to walk as a king, to battle as a warrior—salvation it will bring to those you meet.

"Now to one who works, his wages are not reckoned as a gift but as his due. And to one who does not work but trusts him who justifies the ungodly, his faith is reckoned as righteousness." Romans 4:4-5

The devil I did defeat, but a war continues for each soul.

It is My desire that all would know the Truth, receive My Love, and therefore repent and be saved—as did you. You are now My warrior—empowered.

Super-Naturally

"Fear not, for I am with you, be not dismayed, for I am your God; I will strengthen you, I will help you, I will uphold you with my victorious right hand. Behold, all who are incensed against you shall be put to shame and confounded; those who strive against you shall be as nothing and shall perish. You shall seek those who contend with you, but you shall not find them; those who war against you shall be as nothing at all. For I, the Lord your God, hold your right hand; it is I who say to you, 'Fear not, I will help you.'" Isaiah 41:10-13

"The Lord is the everlasting God, the Creator of the ends of the earth. He does not faint or grow weary, his understanding is unsearchable. He gives power to the faint, and to him who has no might he increases strength. Even youths shall faint and be weary, and young men shall fall exhausted; but they who wait for the Lord shall renew their strength, they shall mount up with wings like eagles, they shall run and not be weary, they shall walk and not faint." Isaiah 40:28-31

"Blessed be the Lord, my rock, who trains my hands for war, and my fingers for battle; my rock and my fortress, my stronghold and my deliverer, my shield and he in whom I take refuge, who subdues the peoples under him." Psalms 144:1-2

~ Hebrews 10:12-17 ~ Luke 24:46-48 ~ Galatians 4:4-7 ~
~ Ephesians 6:10-12 ~

Power You Can't Deny

Sudden destruction will come upon those who deny My Power and choose, rather, to mock and ridicule the anointed.

"Have those who work evil no understanding, who eat up my people as they eat bread, and do not call upon God?" Psalms 53:4

I AM patient, I wait.

But they play with fire and expect not to burn.

Lost souls cry out for deliverance and I AM there.

"Offer to God a sacrifice of thanksgiving, and pay your vows to the Most High; and call upon me in the day of trouble; I will deliver you, and you shall glorify me." Psalms 50:14-15

Hungry hearts long for companionship and I AM there.

I AM patient and kind and I long to comfort but where My Holy Spirit is, there am I also.

If you deny My Power, you deny Me.

"But you shall receive power when the Holy Spirit has come upon you; and you shall be my witnesses in Jerusalem and in all Judea and Samaria and to the end of the earth." Acts 1:8

"Jesus said to them again, 'Peace be with you. As the Father has sent me, even so I send you.' And when he had said this, he breathed on them, and said to them, 'Receive the Holy Spirit.'" John 20:21-22

"And when they had prayed, the place in which they were gathered together was shaken; and they were all filled with the Holy Spirit and spoke the word of God with boldness." Acts 4:31

"And he said to them, "Did you receive the Holy Spirit when you believed?" And they said, "No, we have never even heard that there is a Holy Spirit." And he said, "Into what then were you baptized?" they said. "Into John's baptism." And Paul said, "John baptized with the baptism of repentance, telling the people to believe in the one who was to come after him, that is, Jesus." On hearing this, they were baptized in the name of the Lord Jesus. And when Paul had laid his hands upon them, the Holy Spirit came on them and they spoke with tongues and prophesied." Acts 19:2-6

~ Acts 10:34-38 ~ Acts 10:43-46a ~ Acts 11:15-17 ~

~ Romans 8:26-27 ~

With the Patience of a Saint

I AM prepared to follow through with My Word, but are you prepared for the answer?

The farmer doesn't, one day, prepare for a crop and the next day harvest. He plans, tills, plants, waters, weeds, prays and waits. (James 5:7)

There are many that lose faith when instant answers do not come.

Just as trees grow at different rates—some fast and some very slowly, your answer may not come quickly. But though it may take the tree many years to reach the maturity you seek, that tree is still growing and changing, even as we speak.

So are you.

Sometimes your maturity level is a requirement for the answer to come. Sometimes I wait for you—for the conditions to be right for you to receive.

Sometimes I wait for you to truly believe.

You see, you may speak it with your mouth and think it in your head, but faith is a matter of the heart. When faith flows from your heart and matches the words from your mouth, then you are ready to receive—your harvest will come.

Are you prepared to wait for Me or should I prepare to wait for you? (Psalms 38:15)

Take the steps that you know—increase them as your grow. Be an active participant—in partnership with Me.

Prepare to believe—You will receive!

"Give ear, and hear my voice; hearken, and hear my speech. Does he who plows for sowing plow continually? Does he continually open and harrow his ground? When he has leveled its surface, does he not scatter dill, sow cumin, and put in wheat in rows and barley in its proper place, and spelt as the border? For he is instructed aright; his God teaches him." Isaiah 28:23-26

"My mouth shall speak wisdom; the meditation of my heart shall be understanding." Psalms 49:3

"My son, be attentive to my words; incline your ear to my sayings. Let them not escape from your sight; keep them within your heart. For they are life to him who finds them, and healing to all his flesh. Keep your heart with all vigilance; for from it flow the springs of life." Proverbs 4:20-23

Three Ruptured Disks
A True Testimony

Anyone that has had a disk rupture in their back knows how incredibly painful it is. You can't get out of bed, can't turn, can't move. This may depend on the position and severity of the rupture, but this is how it was in my case—three different times!

The first time it happened, I was working as a banquet waitress at a beautiful and popular resort hotel in another state. We carried trays of plated food up on our shoulders, laden with ten plates of lead china. Each heavy plate held a typical meal of steak, baked potato and broccoli, topped with a stainless-steel cover; above that rested a full pot of coffee, all a great deal of weight.

One day, I lifted that heavy tray and felt my back zing. It was a strange sort of twinge, but not pain. Though I thought it was an odd sensation, I finished out my day. The next day some friends asked me to the movies. I went, not knowing that anything was wrong. By the end of the movie, I was in tears—no longer able to get up; somehow my friends got me up and home, but I am blank as to how they did.

It was a long, arduous ordeal to get well, that involved using a TENS electrical stimulation unit on my back to interrupt the pain. I was treated by a workman's comp doctor; he had me kneel on a four-foot-high wooden stool, and commanded that I lunge forward to touch the floor. I couldn't do it, admittedly, I wouldn't try. I was in so much pain, that it struck terror in my heart at the thought of pitching forth on the floor, and was appalled that he would even suggest such a thing. Consequently, he triumphantly announced that I was making it all up.

No longer able to work, I left the job. My family came to drive me back to Michigan to recover. Back home an MRI, which the work comp doctor had refused to order, showed the rupture. With continuous therapy, my back eventually recovered.

The second time landed me in the hospital for two weeks. I had visited a chiropractor and when I went to pay my bill, was in so much pain after the treatment that I doubled over the desk. I went to my doctor who sent me straight to the hospital. The specialist in the hospital asked me where it hurt. Showing him about six places, he looked at me kind of funny but didn't say much. Later, he came to me to apologize. He told me he had thought I was lying, when I told him all those places it hurt. After seeing the MRI, he said that in 25 years of practice it was the worst rupture he had ever seen. I had a baby, just three months old, but I couldn't hold her. I went home to continue to recover because my baby needed me, but I was still in bed.

I had a paperback Bible of the New Testament next to my bed, that I had just recently purchased at a yard sale. It was a New American Standard, a different version than I was used to. I looked at that Bible and thought to myself, if that was a paperback novel I would read it cover to cover; why not do the same with this Bible? I decided to do that and read it in a week. It was so fulfilling, reading the Word that way. When I finished the last page, I threw up my hands in praise to the Lord; no longer concerned about the pain, but truly thankful that my circumstances had granted me the time to read His Word through.

My back was instantly healed!

The third and final time was another Chiropractor. My doctor sent me to him to work on my neck. Somehow he managed to talk me into adjusting my back. I did not have an issue with my back then, but I left there with my back hurting again. I sought the Lord fervently for healing, but soon became aware that I was seeking the healing more than I was seeking the Lord. With resolve, I told the Lord that He was more important to me than my desire to be healed. I would praise Him no matter what—even if I had to crawl all my days, I would praise Him. Quite dramatic huh? Yes, I was young and it was out of balance, but He got the point; that I loved Him more, even if I did not receive healing. I then said that every time I felt pain, I was going to praise Him.

I followed through, and for three days did a lot of praising.

On the third day I was suddenly healed.

Please don't misunderstand, I am not slamming Chiropractors; I know many have been helped by them. What happened to me began when lifting too much weight to my shoulders. I expect this caused a weakness in my back that was a precursor to future incidents.

My point is this—*three times my back was ruptured and three times I came to be healed.* One incident was by natural means and took a very long time; the other two were miraculous, but the time frame was different in each. There is not a 'formula' to healing, but to seek the Healer, Jesus, who is the Living Word. I have been healed many, many times, for a variety of things and each time is a different story, requiring a fresh measure of faith.

Each story is a testimony that begins and remains IN HIM.

"In him was life, and the life was the light of men." John 1:4

"And all the crowd sought to touch him, for power came forth from him and healed them all." Luke 6:19

Hey, That's Mine

License is given for you to take hold of that which the devil has stolen; be it family and friends or belongings of life, he has no right—lest you be in strife—that is his only authority.

Should you give him priority—

repent.

Turn again to the Word and receive your cleanse.

Do not stay in strife, if you value your life.

For strife will lead you straight downhill. It binds the heart, right from the start—puts blinders on the 'eyes' who see; a deception that binds those who are free. (Ephesians 4:26-27)

"It is an honor for a man to keep aloof from strife; but every fool will be quarreling." Proverbs 20:3

Repent and lay hold of the gift you've been told—that of authority.

For he has no right to the children's delights; *bind him*—take back what you see.

Say . . .

Give it to me!

"Let no evil talk come out of your mouths, but only such as is good for edifying, as fits the occasion, that it may impart grace to those who hear. And do not grieve the Holy Spirit of God, in whom you were sealed for the day of redemption. Let all bitterness and wrath and anger and clamor and slander be put away from you, with all malice, and be kind to one another, tenderhearted, forgiving one another, as God in Christ forgave you." Ephesians 4:29-32

"And he called the twelve together and gave them power and authority over all demons and to cure diseases, and he sent them out to preach the kingdom of God and to heal." Luke 9:1-2

"The seventy returned with joy, saying, 'Lord, even the demons are subject to us in your name!' And he said to them, 'I saw Satan fall like lightening from heaven. Behold, I have given you authority to tread upon serpents and scorpions, and over all the power of the enemy; and nothing shall hurt you. Nevertheless do not rejoice in this, that the spirits are subject to you; but rejoice that your names are written in heaven.'" Luke 10:17-20

"Truly, I say to you, whatever you bind on earth shall be bound in heaven, and whatever you loose on earth shall be loosed in heaven." Matthew 18:18

Be Ready for More

Dramatic changes are coming your way, and you will find it best—

to learn how to rest.

- ❖ Rest in My Provision.
- ❖ Rest in My Wisdom.
- ❖ Rest in My Direction.

All are My Love.

You are never alone—means that, you not only have My companionship but that you literally do nothing alone. My Holy Spirit teaches you from within—where to begin.

"And I will pray the Father, and he will give you another Counselor, to be with you forever, even the Spirit of truth, whom the world cannot receive, because it neither sees him nor knows him; you know him, for he dwells with you, and will be in you." John 14:16-17

Follow-through is an important key.

When you begin—you ask. (John 16:24)

I give you a task.

Don't continue to ask, but work on what I gave you.

So many keep praying, keep asking, but never launch out into the deep for a draught.

Blessing comes in **obedience**—stepping out in faith with what you know—

continuing with more, as you grow.

Peter took the biggest catch of his life and then promptly left it to follow Me. You see, it's not about the 'catch,' but the direction that I call you to—

the catch will follow you as you go.

You are not pursuing a lifestyle, you are pursuing Me, and a Kingdom—My style. I will give you all you need and more, as you continue to open each door, and *follow—*

Follow My lead.

"If anyone serves me, he must follow me; and where I am, there shall my servant be also; if anyone serves me, the Father will honor him." John 12:26

Shall we proceed?

Be ready for more.

So much more!

"Now when he had left speaking, he said unto Simon, launch out into the deep, and let down your nets for a draught. And Simon answering said unto him, Master, we have toiled all the night, and have taken nothing; nevertheless at thy word I will let down the net. And when they had this done, they enclosed a great multitude of fishes; and their net brake. And they beckoned unto their partners, which were in the other ship, that they should come and help them. And they came, and filled both ships, so that they began to sink. When Simon Peter saw it, he fell down at Jesus' knees, saying, Depart from me; for I am a sinful man, O Lord. For he was astonished, and all that were with him, at the draught of the fishes which they had taken: And so was also James, and John, the sons of Zebedee, which were partners with Simon. And Jesus said unto Simon, Fear not; from henceforth thou shalt catch men. And when they had brought their ships to land, they forsook all, and followed him." Luke 5:4-11 KJV

What Limit?

The density of My Word is determined by how you perceive it.

One might say I AM very shallow, for I would not fight. Another would say I AM very deep, for they cannot understand My Word. Both are true statements *for them*, for they know *very little* of Me. Therefore, their perception is small and this becomes *their* truth.

I AM as much truth as man is willing to accept, for I AM immeasurable and unending.

Therefore, you may explore Me and never reach a final conclusion.

Think on that.

So, when you *define* who I AM, think again.

"—that according to the riches of his glory he may grant you to be strengthened with might through his Spirit in the inner man, and that Christ may dwell in your hearts through faith; that you, being rooted and grounded in love, may have power to comprehend with all the saints what is the breadth and length and height and depth, and to know the love of Christ which surpasses knowledge, that you may be filled with all the fulness of God." Ephesians 3:16-19

And when you think that there is a limit in your life—

think again.

Who put that limit there?

Do you really think that I, a limitless God, who created you in My image, would choose to limit you?

"So God created man in his own image, in the image of God he created him; male and female he created them. And God blessed them, and God said to them, 'Be fruitful and multiply, and fill the earth and subdue it; and have dominion over the fish of the sea and over the birds of the air and over every living thing that moves upon the earth.'" Genesis 1:27-28

You—you only, limit yourself.

Therefore, I AM asking that you change your perception of you, by changing your perception of Me.

Know Me more, that you may know more.

There is so much more, if *in* you—you can *see* Me.

"I do not cease to give thanks for you, remembering you in my prayers, that the God of our Lord Jesus Christ, the Father of glory, may give you a spirit of wisdom and a revelation in the knowledge of him, having the eyes of your hearts enlightened, that you may know what is the hope to which he has called you, what are the riches of his glorious inheritance in the saints, and what is the immeasurable greatness of his power in us who believe, according to the working of his great might which he accomplished in Christ when he raised him from the dead and made him sit at his right hand in heavenly places, far above all rule and authority and power and dominion, and above every name that is named, not only in this age but also in that which is to come; and he has put all things under his feet and has made him the head over all things for the church which is the body, the fulness of him who fills all in all." Ephesians 1:16-23

"And God gave Solomon wisdom and understanding beyond measure, and largeness of mind like the sand on the seashore, so that Solomon's wisdom surpassed the wisdom of all the people of the east, and all the wisdom of Egypt." I Kings 4:29-30

"Now to him who by the power at work within us is able to do far more abundantly than all that we ask or think, to him be glory in the church and in Christ Jesus to all generations, for ever and ever. Amen." Ephesians 3:20-21

Toby
A True Testimony

When in my early twenties, I lived alone in a tiny house that just seemed to be a little too quiet. I was missing a little black Miniature Schnauzer dog named Toby, that I no longer had.

The rule where I lived was "NO PETS," but I spoke to the Lord about it and asked Him if He would convince my landlord otherwise. I confidently approached the landlord that afternoon to ask if I could have a dog; his response was favorable. I thanked him, but clarified that I was just thinking about it, and that it likely wouldn't happen right away. Apparently though, the Lord already had my desire on His heart, when I prayed, because the answer was already in process.

The next day, when sitting in my living room, I heard a car pull up to my mailbox to deliver the paper. This was a free circulation that consisted of local happenings, ads, and classifieds. The Lord then clearly spoke to my heart, "Go get the paper," He said. "Your dog is in it."

Immediately, I jumped up and ran out the door. I was so excited! The first ad my eyes fell on was that of a black, Miniature Schnauzer for sale, $75.00. It amazes me to this day that, at the same time, He must have given me a gift of faith, because it just didn't occur to me that I didn't have enough money. I literally had only $15.00, no credit cards and no other money in the bank. I lived pretty much hand-to-mouth, by faith. With no thought of lack, I called the woman and told her that I wanted the dog. She agreed to meet me at my work, in the parking lot at 9:30 that night, to make the exchange.

So excited, I went to work that day telling everyone that would listen, about the dog I was getting that night. At lunch break, I related to my co-workers that I needed a cage, because the dog was a nine-month old puppy and I didn't want him chewing up my antiques when I was at work. A co-worker responded that she had one, and would sell it to me for $15.00.

Now I hadn't told anyone how much money I had, but it was perfect— I had just enough! She lived nearby, so she went home and got it for me. Now I owned a cage, but had no money, and my dog was coming in a matter of a few hours. It just didn't occur to me to panic, for I had heard from God and that thought just never crossed my mind. Instead, I continued excitedly telling everyone around that I was getting a dog—tonight!

As a banquet waitress for a large hotel, we often worked what we called a 'double shift,' which was working two different parties in the same day. This day I was to work both lunch and dinner, but everyone else went home after the lunch shift.

The manager's office was located just before a freezer and dry storage room. As I passed by, the manager leaned out his door to greet me. "Oh, Hi Lori," he said. "Are you the only one here?" he asked, peering down the hall past me. When I nodded affirmation he continued, "Well, I guess you can have yours now." With that he invited me into his office and handed me a long, plain envelope. Now this was the month of June—summertime! Grinning a little sheepishly he clarified, "This is your Christmas bonus," adding, "We never got them out last year." With a huge smile, I thanked him and continued on, later to discover that the envelope contained a check for $150.00—Wow!

My bank was conveniently located one block from the hotel, so I was able to cash the check on my dinner break. It was more than enough for my new puppy. When he came to meet me, I called him Toby and he came to me as if that had always been his name. When we arrived home, he raced around investigating every room, then came and laid on my foot and went to sleep. He was home. Who ever heard of a Christmas bonus in June? I think that was God's idea! When God decides, He provides! It was double what I needed, but then He knew I would need dog food and toys—He is a God of more than enough!

Just Us

An audience of one, that's all I ask of you. I work with you as an individual, personally. Our relationship should be just that—personal.

I trust that you want to know My Heart, as I know yours.

The difference is, I know you completely and you can never know all that I AM.

I AM too vast for the human mind to perceive. Therefore, I ask you to know Me with your heart; follow who I AM and believe. It's simple to start, but the more you grow, the deeper you go into My Heart—the more you grow.

"I will give them a heart to know that I am the Lord; and they shall be my people and I will be their God, for they shall return to me with their whole heart." Jeremiah 24:7

It is like a deep, deep well that becomes deeper the more you drink; likewise, the more you drink, the clearer you see how much more you have to drink. You will thirst no more, in that you will be satisfied—you've found the Truth.

"Jesus said to her, 'Everyone who drinks of this water will thirst again, but whoever drinks of the water that I shall give him will never thirst; the water that I shall give him will become in him a spring of water welling up to eternal life." John 4:13-14

Water is a universal substance necessary to life, that is still free. Rich or poor, all can partake, all can find a source of water to maintain life.

All can partake of Me.

I AM Free.

I AM Life.

"Ho, everyone who thirsts, come to the waters; and he who has no money, come, buy and eat! Come, buy wine and milk without money and without price." Isaiah 55:1

Come to Me, an audience of one. If you ask for a drink, I will give freely the Water of Life that you may thirst no more.

But ever live to drink again—More!

"With joy you will draw water from the wells of salvation." Isaiah 12:3

"How precious is thy steadfast love, O God! The children of men take refuge in the shadow of thy wings. They feast on the abundance of thy house, and thou givest them drink from the river of thy delights. For with thee is the fountain of life; in thy light do we see light." Psalms 36:7-9

Built for Worship

You read of the elaborate house Solomon built for Me; it does not begin to compare to thee. How do silver, gold, jewels and the like, carry the price of a human life? (II Chronicles 2:5-6)

That house was built to worship Me, how much more I'd ask that you bow before Me, least once each day; to ask and pray for the lost, the lonely, those broken of heart; the ones that never had a start—for sin took their life.

Please pray for those left behind, to bear the pain, suffering and shame of a choice not right; maiden flight—stolen in the night, a heart too freely give.

Please bow thy knee, entreat of Me to come, to mend the heart clearly numb . . .

I'll come.

I'll come.

Each house is built to worship Me—a project only God could see—for the human mind could not devise, the intricacy of body, spirit, and soul, placed together to make one whole. A spirit inclined toward the divine—the missing key, to fill the hole of a heart that's not complete.

Please pray for that one, that hungry soul.

Please bow and ask that they might know, that I can make it alright.

I'll come.

I'll come.

The house was built for worship; a costlier one had never been built—*until there was you*—nothing compares to you!

Not gold, not silver—just you.

Worship and pray.

I will come!

"If my people who are called by my name humble themselves, and pray and seek my face, and turn from their wicked ways, then I will hear from heaven, and will forgive their sin and heal their land. Now my eyes will be open and my ears attentive to the prayer that is made in this place. For now, I have chosen and consecrated this house that my name may be there forever; my eyes and my heart will be there for all time." II Chronicles 7:14-16

"—and the prayer of faith will save the sick man, and the Lord will raise him up; and if he has committed sins, he will be forgiven. Therefore, confess your sins to one another, and pray for one another, that you may be healed. The prayer of a righteous man has great power in its effects." James 5:15-16

"And you, Solomon my son, know the God of your father, and serve him with a whole heart and with a willing mind; for the Lord searches all hearts, and understands every plan and thought. If you seek him, he will be found by you; but if you forsake him, he will cast you off forever." I Chronicles 28:9

Royal Destiny

There is a great stirring of My people across the land; an agitated enemy arising to face those who serve the Lamb, in a final attempt to bring fear and destruction. Those who know My Word have no fear— their destination is clear, and they will not be thwarted nor derailed.

This is not a time for a child to continue on milk and soft foods.

You must be weaned quickly, for as the days grow colder, the chill in the air foretells of an increasing coldness in the hearts of man.

"And because wickedness is multiplied, most men's love will grow cold. But he who endures to the end will be saved. And this gospel of the kingdom will be preached throughout the whole world, as a testimony to all nations; and then the end will come." Matthew 24:12-14

The time has come for sides to be drawn.

Intermingling will not be tolerated; for as the days of the times wax shorter, it is expedient that all declare allegiance to the God they serve, or it will be the 'god' they serve. A somber note for a generation adept at avoiding the Truth. (Malachi 4:1-3)

Salt is good, but if it has lost its saltiness of what use is it but to be thrown out and trampled on by men? (Matthew 5:13)

You must find your place, be seasoned in Grace, as these latter days wind to an end.

"Conduct yourselves wisely toward outsiders, making the most of the time. Let your speech always be gracious, seasoned with salt, so that you may know how you ought to answer everyone." Colossians 4:5-6

But you, My friend, are hidden from My Face—the wrath that must take place—the judgment to come upon all. For those who have found their place, set apart from the human race, are *Royal Destiny* awaiting the Throne. (Revelation 6:15-17) (Malachi 3:16-18)

Take a side—choose to abide.

"But you are not in darkness, brethren, for that day to surprise you like a thief. For you are all sons of light and sons of the day; we are not of the night or of darkness. So then let us not sleep, as others do, but let us keep awake and be sober." I Thessalonians 5:4-6

"For God has not destined us for wrath, but to obtain salvation through our Lord Jesus Christ, who died for us so that whether we wake or sleep we might live with him." I Thessalonians 5:9-10

"He who dwells in the shelter of the Most High, who abides in the shadow of the Almighty, will say to the Lord, 'My refuge and my fortress; my God, in whom I trust.'" "Because he cleaves to me in love, I will deliver him; I will protect him, because he knows my name. When he calls to me, I will answer him; I will be with him in trouble, I will rescue him and honor him. With long life I will satisfy him, and show him my salvation." Psalms 91:1-2, 14-16

~ I John 2:28-29 ~

End-time Prophecy

Heard in my Spirit, Approximately 2004

There is going to be a great ROAR!

It will happen so suddenly it will shake the world. It is the roar of the Lion of the Tribe of Judah! It will be the roar of Jesus, coming out of His uncompromised church—the remnant; who know Him and His ways, not only from the Word, but by His Spirit. (Amos 3:7-8)

Those who are unbending and refuse to make excuses for the world and its ways; they are preparing now and, if you are one of them, you sense it. You are already anticipating this great move of God, in readiness.

This ROAR will happen so suddenly it will stop evil in its tracks for a brief time, as if stunned.

The true church will take back the authority that is rightfully hers and the dead church will fall.

A great out-pouring of declaration will come forth like never before. Bold, strong Christians will rise up, proudly and loudly proclaiming the supremacy of Jesus!

It will be an exhilarating and exciting time, a time of freedom and celebration. Make much of this time, for though it will seem unending, it will be short and brief; for the enemy will again get a footing and will then rise up more vile and darker than ever before.

This powerful declaration will usher in the final persecution of the church; many will give their lives for Christ. It is the final battle, where sides must be taken. No more compromise will be tolerated. All must choose whom they will serve and serve they will.

This must take place. It is the platform that will usher in our Glorious and Triumphant Coming King!

Come Lord Jesus!

Sustained Peace

Unusual changes will be seen on the Earth. My message will be heard in ways not expected and not sought after.

For there are many who refuse to acknowledge the Truth, even though it is written plainly, clearly, in bold black and white; still they close their eyes—stop their ears and refuse to see—listen—refuse to acknowledge that I AM their Creator, even though I love them so. Therefore, I must strike their attention in ways they will not be able to avoid.

Strange happenings and phenomena will occur that will make men wonder and cause them to stop and exclaim. Those who have refused the Truth will have no foundation on which to stand, and no stronghold on which to cling—their confidence will be shaken.

Have I gotten their attention?

It will only be the beginning.

For as My Word states, I will cause a delusion for they have refused the Truth. Never turn your back on My Truth. It is your strong defense in times of trouble and unrest, the likes of which man has not yet known in this present age.

I urge you to study My Word, faithfully, to be prepared for these end-time trials. For they are soon to begin, and I would have all My children to be prepared and always confident.

For My Word dwells within you.

And,

If that be true, confident you will remain and . . .

your peace it will sustain!

"For the mystery of lawlessness is already at work; only he who now restrains it will do so until he is out of the way. And then the lawless one will be revealed, and the Lord Jesus will slay him with the breath of his mouth and destroy him by his appearing and his coming. The coming of the lawless one by the activity of Satan will be with all power and with pretended signs and wonders, and with all wicked deception for those who are to perish, because they refused to love the truth and so be saved. Therefore, God sends upon them a strong delusion, to make them believe what is false, so that all may be condemned who did not believe the truth but had pleasure in unrighteousness." II Thessalonians 2:7-12

"—for it is written, 'As I live, says the Lord, every knee shall bow to me, and every tongue shall give praise to God.' So each of us shall give account of himself to God." Romans 14:11-12

Author's Note: This message was originally posted on April 3, 2013. The same day, as if in confirmation, it snowed hard in the afternoon but the temperature outside was 54 degrees.

Waiting for Vindication

It is good and right for the upright to see My vindication on their enemies, for it satisfies justice.

"Vindicate me, O Lord, for I have walked in my integrity, and I have trusted in the Lord without wavering. Prove me, O Lord, and try me; test my heart and my mind. For thy steadfast love is before my eyes, and I walk in faithfulness to thee." Psalms 26:1-3

Some of you have waited many years for this satisfaction.

But do you wait for bad things to happen to them—much as if I would rub their nose in the dirt to punish?

No, I say, that is not My desire. It is for you that I wait.

I wait for your heart to turn.

I wait for you to love in forgiveness and understand that it is not My desire to harm, but to build.

"Hatred stirs up strife, but love covers all offenses." Proverbs 10:12

My desire is to build you before your enemy, but can I do this when you have bitterness and unforgiveness in your heart?

It is for you I wait.

Learn to love those who don't love you, for that is who I AM.

Do this, and I will lift you to a position that you no longer care what your enemy has done.

Because, for you—

Life has begun!

"The Lord works vindication and justice for all who are oppressed. He made known his ways to Moses, his acts to the people of Israel. The Lord is merciful and gracious, slow to anger and abounding in steadfast love. He will not always chide, nor will he keep his anger forever. He does not deal with us according to our sins, nor requite us according to our iniquities. For as the heavens are high above the earth, so great is his steadfast love toward those who fear him; as far as the east is from the west, so far does he remove our transgression from us. As a father pities his children, so the Lord pities those who fear him. For he knows our frame; he remembers that we are dust." Psalms 103:6-14

"When a man's ways please the Lord, he makes even his enemies to be at peace with him." Proverbs 16:7

"Thou preparest a table before me in the presence of my enemies; thou anointest my head with oil, my cup overflows." Psalms 23:5

Turn and See

My heart cries out for the lost.

My heart cries out for those who have heard the Good News and yet they turn a deaf ear, as if they have a choice. They do, but is there any comparison between My love and the devil?

"Woe to those who call evil good and good evil, who put darkness for light and light for darkness, who put bitter for sweet and sweet for bitter! Woe to those who are wise in their own eyes, and shrewd in their own sight!" Isaiah 5:20-21

For the earth will be filled with My Glory and then where will they stand?

How will they stand?

They see so much, hear so much, and yet they do not see—they do not hear; they have stopped up their ears. They refuse to listen and have turned their back to the coming King.

Oh, but I love them; how I long for them to hear My call—to turn from wickedness and see . . .

- ❖ That their lives are empty.
- ❖ They have need of a Savior.
- ❖ Their world is coming to a close.

And there comes a time when there will be no more time.

Oh, turn and see, that your Savior is Me.

I AM Jesus!

Come

"I was ready to be sought by those who did not ask for Me; I was ready to be found by those who did not seek Me. I said, 'Here am I,' to a nation that did not call My name." Isaiah 65:1

"The Lord is just in all His ways, and kind in all His doings. The Lord is near to all who call upon Him, to all who call upon Him in truth. He fulfills the desire of all who fear Him, He also hears their cry, and saves them. The Lord preserves all who love Him; but all the wicked He will destroy." Psalms 145:17-20

The Extra Mile

Clamor and evil speaking must cease. For if you are willing to follow Me, then you must be willing to think like Me, speak like Me. In loving your neighbor as yourself, you submit to that person's heart, conceding that you will care for it as your own; for no one ever hated his own flesh, but nourishes and cares for it. (Ephesians 5:29-30)

Will you—

go the extra mile to care for the heart of a friend?

How about the heart of one you don't even know?

I created him too, will you love him even as you love Me? *I expect this from you*, just as you expect Me to care for you—

and I do

Oh, I really do—care for you!

"This is the message we have heard from him and proclaim to you, that God is light and in him is no darkness at all. If we say we have fellowship with him while we walk in darkness, we lie and do not live according to the truth; but if we walk in the light, as he is in the light, we have fellowship with one another, and the blood of Jesus his Son cleanses us from all sin." I John 1:5-7

"For no man ever hates his own flesh, but nourishes and cherishes it, as Christ does the church, because we are members of his body." Ephesians 5:29-30

"We who are strong ought to bear with the failings of the weak, and not to please ourselves; let each of us please his neighbor for his good, to edify him." Romans 15:1-2

Tara's Healing
A True Testimony

Several years ago, a woman I worked with (I'll call her Tara) asked me to pray for her. She wanted healing of Rheumatoid Arthritis. Recalling that incident, I admit that I didn't feel encouraged to jump right in and pray for her. Healing is the believers' Covenant right; a child of God may stand on the Word and expect to be healed. My understanding was that she was not a believer. Therefore, I was concerned that it might not happen and send her further away from God. If I remember correctly, three different times she asked me to pray, each time I urged that **she** pray. I just wasn't finding confidence in my heart, so I prayed in private and waited on God for instruction.

One very early morning, many weeks later, the Lord woke me up with instruction to read a certain Scripture. After that came another, and then another. I read and recorded them and it was then, after all those weeks, that He spoke to my heart . . .

"Today is the day to pray for (Tara), I'm going to heal her."

Now I had **heard** from God and was released to pray. "Take anointing oil with you to work," and with that, He settled the quest.

Tara held the door for me that morning, which was unusual, for it had never happened before that she was the first person that greeted me. Excited and smiling I asked, "Do you still want prayer?" She instantly lit up and exclaimed, "Yes!" "God's going to heal you today!" I told her, assuredly. Right behind us, her best friend walked in. I asked her if she would join us later to pray. She was nervous, but agreed. We met in the bathroom on break. It was an odd place to pray, but I wanted the privacy. So, at 9:00 am, Tara sat on a stool in the bathroom. After applying anointing oil, we **tried** to lay hands on her. The friend and I had no more than lifted our hands to do so, when the Fire of God came down so HOT that we couldn't touch her. With tears streaming down all three of our faces, Tara leaped off the stool — instantly healed! It all happened so fast that her friend and I were speechless. Tara sailed out of the bathroom with a huge smile on her face, declaring, "I'm healed!" Pausing just outside the open doorframe, she did a twirl, turned and looked back at me, announcing, "You didn't know this but, today is my birthday!"

I didn't know it was her birthday, but God did.
Tara told me the next day that she had gone home and rode her horse for the first time in two years.

Praise Jesus for His healing power! I felt it was lack of faith that I didn't pray for her right away, but maybe God didn't give me the confidence to pray because He wanted her to have a special birthday surprise. His timing is perfect, if we wait on Him. This extra special day *especially* spoke to Tara, that God knows and cares about her personally—*He knows her birthday*!

Tara was eager to pray for another co-worker after experiencing her own healing. In going together to pray for another, I was privileged to witness Tara ask the Lord into her heart. ♡

Sittin' on a Log

If I could just see to get that log out of my eye, I am confident that I will find that my brother doesn't have the speck that I thought he had—*it is merely the shadow of my own log.*

"Why do you see that speck that is in your brother's eye, but do not notice the log that is in your own eye? Or how can you say to your brother, 'Let me take the speck out of your eye,' when there is a log in your own eye? You hypocrite, first take the log out of your own eye, and then you will see clearly to take the speck out of your brother's eye." Matthew 7:3-5

Why can't I seem to get that log out?

I think my fingers are too big or pointed in the wrong direction. I will look to the Word. I am sure therein is the tool to remove the log from my eye.

When I've got that log out, I will see clearly to *love my neighbor as myself.*

For I am certain to be more loveable then!

"And he said to him, 'You shall love the Lord your God with all your heart, and with all your soul, and with all your mind. This is the great and first commandment. And a second is like it, you shall love your neighbor as yourself. On these two commandments depend all the law and the prophets.'" Matthew 22:37-40

Against All Odds

Against all odds you became saved, for it is not in your nature to seek good and shun evil. My children were created pure and holy . . .

Then came sin.

Sin separated man from the Father, and created a new nature and environment for his life . . .

- ❖ The garden was no longer perfect.
- ❖ Trust was broken.
- ❖ Weeds entered in.
- ❖ Tears were shed.

But, I had a plan from the very beginning. To reinstate man into My Grace, I asked My Son to take your place.

Against all odds,

God became a man, born of a natural woman, to sever the divide . . .

Mary agreed.

Jesus became.

But yet, there was more to come . . .

For you were born into the natural world, where sin still reigned. Without a Savior, there is no hope. A choice has to be made for man to be under the rule of God and not man. To have dominion, and to rule and reign, one must choose the *great exchange.*

Your old life, for one that is completely FREE—never again held to the lie of shame. Your life renewed—never to die again. Your spirit forever shall live and ever with Me you'll remain. Where there is no more sorrow, sadness, or pain—a perfect garden, no weeds—*all gain.*

Your answer then, was it against all odds that you said yes?

- ❖ Yes to Jesus?
- ❖ Yes to Love?
- ❖ Yes to Life?

Yes, against all odds—Welcome Home Son—Welcome Home Daughter—

Welcome Home!

Have you invited your friends? There is *always* room for more . . .

Against all Odds.

"And as Moses lifted up the serpent in the wilderness, so must the Son of man be lifted up, that whoever believes in him may have eternal life. For God so loved the world that he gave his only Son, that whoever believes in him should not perish but have eternal life. For God sent the Son into the world, not to condemn the world, but that the world might be saved through him. He who believes in him is not condemned; he who does not believe in condemned already, because he has not believed in the name of the only Son of God. And this is the judgment that the light has come into the world, and men loved darkness rather than light, because their deeds were evil. For everyone who does evil hates the light, and does not come to the light, lest his deeds be exposed. But he who does what is true comes to the light, that it may be clearly seen that his deeds have been wrought in God." John 3:14-21

"In him was life, and the life was the light of men. The light shines in darkness, and the darkness has not overcome it." John 1:4-5

"Jesus answered him, 'Truly, truly, I say to you, unless one is born anew, he cannot see the kingdom of God.'" John 3:3

"But the hour is coming, and now is, when the true worshipers will worship the Father in spirit and truth, for such the Father seeks to worship him. God is spirit, and those who worship him must worship in spirit and truth. The woman said to him, 'I know that Messiah is coming, (he who is called Christ); when he comes, he will show us all things.' Jesus said to her, 'I who speak to you am he.'" John 4:23-26

A Twinkle in Your Eye

Do you suppose Abraham wondered about the grains of sand and the stars in the sky? It is a hard thing to fathom, something so far-fetched, and yet to believe—*but he did!* (Genesis 15:1,5-6)

"I will indeed bless you, and I will multiply your descendants as the stars of heaven and as the sand which is on the seashore." Genesis 22:17a

He believed the impossible to be possible and it became.

Faith like that triumphs! That faith receives . . .

Do you believe?

Accept as fact, that which has no facts, just because I told you so.

When you trust Me that much, the sky holds no limit—

just as Abraham found to receive.

The stars that do shine, are a twinkle in His eye—*an endless family.*

I want you to seek Me for the outrageous plan in your life—believe Me for that which cannot be done.

For I AM the God who doesn't know impossible—

I speak, and so it is done!

Call upon Me, while I am near.

Come to Me without fear.

I invite you to come, and we will discuss your future—*if you are willing to dream.* For I have a plan—*it is unlike another,* for each one is individual to Me.

So, come to Me, all who are willing to try, that which never has been done.

For I AM creative 'always'.

Make no mistake—

I finish what hasn't begun!

"And Jesus said to him, 'If you can! All things are possible to him who believes.'" Mark 9:23

"Jesus looked at them and said, 'With men it is impossible, but not with God; for all things are possible with God.'" Mark 10:27

"And without faith it is impossible to please him. For whoever would draw near to God must believe that he exists and that he rewards those who seek him." Hebrews 11:6

"O give thanks to the Lord, call on his name, make known his deeds among the peoples! Sing to him, sing praises to him, tell of all his wonderful works! Glory in his holy name; let the hearts of those who seek the Lord rejoice! Seek the Lord and his strength, seek his presence continually! Remember the wonderful works that he has done, his miracles, and the judgments he uttered, O offspring of Abraham his servant, sons of Jacob, his chosen ones!" Psalms 105:1-6

"Know therefore that the Lord your God is God, the faithful God who keeps covenant and steadfast love with those who love him and keep his commandments—" Deuteronomy 7:9

Walk Free

Blessed is the man who keeps My council, who walks in the way of righteousness. His foot will not slip, for if you have been made righteous by My Blood, I AM the keeper of your steps. (Psalms 37:30-31)

Your life is hidden within Me, and in My Light you shall see light and more light and more . . .

I will increase your light, as you take delight in the light you've been given.

Those who have chosen to walk in My steps, shall not again walk in darkness for My Light casts darkness away from them.

Light consumes darkness and overpowers it.

Delight in My ways and in giving Me praise, so your days will be filled with laughter, and the joy of the Lord is your strength! (Psalms 126:1-6) (Nehemiah 8:10)

Much heartache can be found by those who **seem** profound, but are speaking against My Word. They call into being things lacking—**not seeing** the power that's spoken in My Word. (Ephesians 5:6-14)

So trust Me at all times, looking forward—not back, the times becoming increasingly clear; that it's My Voice you should hear, and not that in your ear—

of the enemy calling you back.

Come forward into My fullness of joy!

Don't look back, to that of lack, for I take great delight in giving you light, that poverty you'll no longer see.

By faith you shall walk FREE!

"How precious is thy steadfast love, O God! The children of men take refuge in the shadow of thy wings. They feast on the abundance of thy house, and thou givest them drink from the river of thy delights. For with thee is the fountain of life; in thy light do we see light." Psalms 36:7-9

"The angel of the Lord encamps around those who fear him, and delivers them. O taste and see that the Lord is good! Happy is the man who takes refuge in Him! O fear the Lord, you his saints, for those who fear him have no want! The young lions suffer want and hunger; but those who seek the Lord lack no good thing." Psalms 34:7-10

"Thou dost show me the path of life; in thy presence there is fulness of joy, in thy right hand are pleasures for evermore." Psalms 16:11

About the Author

Lori O'Neil writes from a heart that listens. If you speak to her of her books, she is quick to respond that they are God's messages and she simply takes dictation.

"The Lord asked me to write a blog several years ago," she states "I agreed to, but didn't know how to begin. Within two days someone approached me and initiated a conversation about a blog. From that conversation, I learned how to launch and maintain a blog, that He then **filled** with messages. In the fall of 2014, He asked me to write a book. I consented, but soon found myself in a battle for my husband's life, which precipitated my own journey to restoration. We don't always have control over the adversity that life brings us; but we do have a choice to react or respond. Like many humans, I reacted, but then took the steps to respond—to Him!"

In Lori's first book, 'Comfort in the Challenge,' she fulfilled God's request to write a book, His book. In it you may read how God sent her to Israel, performed three miracles, and connected her to a publisher. As she began that book, prisoners, rose up in her heart so strong; and greater yet, His Compassion!

'His Voice in My Heart' is Lori's second published book and the first in a three-volume set. She writes from the Heart of Compassion of the one who **is** Compassion—He is Love!

Lori O'Neil is a native of Michigan. She lives near Traverse City with her dog Houston and authors the blog, www.wordscroll.org.

Thank you for selecting

'His Voice in My Heart'

We welcome your comments.

Send correspondence to:

P.O. Box 22, Acme, MI 49610

Please understand, due to the volume of mail,

we are unable to respond to every letter received.

God Bless you, Lori O'Neil

Books by

Lori J. O'Neil

"Comfort in the Challenge"

Additional copies of this book

Other books in progress

are available at

www.nationofwomenpublishing.com

Nation of Women
PUBLISHING